Academic Success

Applying Learning Theory in the Classroom

Marie Menna Pagliaro

ROWMAN & LITTLEFIELD EDUCATION
A division of
ROWMAN & LITTLEFIELD PUBLISHERS, INC.
Lanham • New York • Toronto • Plymouth, UK

Published by Rowman & Littlefield Education
A division of Rowman & Littlefield Publishers, Inc.
A wholly owned subsidiary of The Rowman & Littlefield Publishing Group, Inc.
4501 Forbes Boulevard, Suite 200, Lanham, Maryland 20706
www.rowman.com

10 Thornbury Road, Plymouth PL6 7PP, United Kingdom

Copyright © 2013 by Marie Menna Pagliaro

All rights reserved. No part of this book may be reproduced in any form or by any electronic or mechanical means, including information storage and retrieval systems, without written permission from the publisher, except by a reviewer who may quote passages in a review.

British Library Cataloguing in Publication Information Available

Library of Congress Cataloging-in-Publication Data

Pagliaro, Marie Menna, 1934-
Academic success : applying learning theory in the classroom / Marie Menna Pagliaro.
p. cm.
Includes bibliographical references.
ISBN 978-1-4758-0569-7 (cloth : alk. paper) -- ISBN 978-1-4758-0570-3 (pbk. : alk. paper) -- ISBN 978-1-4758-0571-0 (electronic)
1. Learning, Psychology of. 2. Cognitive learning. 3. Motivation in education. 4. Academic achievement. I. Title.
LB1060.P34 2014
370.15'23--dc23

2013024630

Also by Marie Menna Pagliaro

Mastery Teaching Skills: A Resource for Implementing the Common Core State Standards
(Rowman & Littlefield, 2012)

Research-Based Unit and Lesson Planning: Maximizing Student Achievement
(Rowman & Littlefield, 2012)

Exemplary Classroom Questioning: Practices To Promote Thinking and Learning
(Rowman & Littlefield, 2011)

Educator or Bully? Managing the 21st Century Classroom
(Rowman & Littlefield, 2011)

Differentiating Instruction: Matching Strategies with Objectives
(Rowman & Littlefield, 2011)

If your principal accused you of being a highly effective teacher, would there be enough evidence to convict you?

Contents

Preface	ix
Introduction	xiii
1 Before You Begin	1
2 Setting the Tone for Learning in Your 21st Century Classroom	5
3 Securing and Maintaining Student Motivation	15
4 Setting Goals/Objectives and Obtaining Feedback	33
5 Engaging Students in New Learning	47
6 Strengthening and Deepening New Learning	79
Appendix A: Involving Students in Active Learning: A Case Study	97
References	105
About the Author	111

Preface

There is no question that teacher effectiveness is the most significant factor affecting student achievement. The positive results of teacher effectiveness have been documented consistently over the past 25 years, beginning with a study led by William Sanders, a statistician at the University of Tennessee, and reported by Sanders and Rivers (1996).

In 1992, the state of Tennessee commissioned Dr. Sanders to analyze the teaching performance of its 30,000 teachers and the records of its 6 million students. In an interview conducted with Marks (2000), Dr. Sanders explained how he and his team examined class size; school location (rural, urban, suburban); ethnicity; students heterogeneously and homogeneously grouped; amount of expenditure per pupil; and percentage of students eligible for free lunch. Much to his surprise, he discovered that *teacher effectiveness* is 10 to 20 times as significant as any of these other factors. He was able to quantify just how much teachers matter and demonstrate that a "bad" teacher can deter the progress of a child for at least four years.

Wright, Horn, and Sanders (1997), in a subsequent study involving 60,000 students, came to the same conclusions. As a result, they recommended that *the best way to improve education is to improve teacher effectiveness.*

Sanders and his colleagues were not the only researchers to emphasize the importance of the teacher's performance on student achievement. The National Commission on Teaching and America's Future (NCTAF) (1996) issued its influential report which indicated that what teachers know and can do is the most important influence on student learning. Haycock (1998), working in Boston and Dallas, reported similar findings, with effective teachers having a profound influence. Pipho (1998) documented that the effectiveness of the individual classroom teacher was the single largest factor affecting student growth, with prior achievement, heterogeneity, and class size paling in comparison with teacher performance. After studying in-service training and district innovations, Joyce and Showers (2002) determined that the key to the growth of students is the growth of teachers.

A study by Felch, Song, and Poindexter (2010) indicated that despite increasing school safety, requiring uniforms, changing the curriculum, offering after-school programs, reducing class size, and increasing a lot more spending per pupil, the **only** progress that came in a chronically underperforming middle school was bringing in effective teachers.

Hanushek (2011), in his own analysis, concluded that an effective teacher, which he defines as one in the top 15 percent for performance based on student achievement, can in one year take an average student from the 50th to the 58th percentile or above. The implication is that the same student with a teacher in the bottom 15 percent will end up below the 42nd percentile. And when assigned a teacher in the bottom 5 percent, a student in the middle of the distribution could fall to the bottom third by the end of the school year.

Hanushek's research also took into account student backgrounds and initial knowledge, and applies to urban, suburban, and rural schools. He even goes on to calculate the economic impact of effective and ineffective teaching. Hanushek concluded that in *a single year*, teachers in the top 15 percent of quality can add at least $20,000 of income throughout a student's life. In a class of 20 students, this teacher can add $400,000 yearly to the economy. On the other side of the coin, teachers in the lowest 15 percent can reduce this same amount *yearly* from the economy.

Economic and academic gains were not the only positive effects of excellent teaching. A study conducted with 2.5 million students over a 20-year period at Columbia and Harvard universities demonstrated that effective teachers also had an effect on increasing college matriculation and reducing teenage pregnancies (Chetty, Friedman, & Rockoff, 2012).

Since the focus in education is currently more on students than on schools, there has now been a corresponding shift to understanding *how* every student can learn well (Stansbury, 2008). Some questions that arise are: How can teachers ensure that they are effective? What should they do in the classroom that makes the difference between students who learn and those who do not? What should teachers do to keep their students actively and meaningfully engaged? These are the questions discussed in this book.

The best way to develop effective teaching skills is to concentrate on how students learn. To ensure that instruction is as effective and efficient as possible, it is imperative that teachers are thoroughly familiar with the basic learning theories. These principles should be integrated into all aspects of instructional planning and delivery.

Moreover, since teachers are not technicians but professionals, they should not only understand the theory that informs their practice, but more important, know how to *apply* that theory in the classroom. Then teachers must **actually implement** what they know and can do.

Learning that is not applied is inert learning, for knowledge of learning theory becomes useful only when it can be turned into performance. Developing more effective teachers by helping them facilitate the implementation of learning theory in the classroom is the focus of this book.

Teacher effectiveness is more important than ever. We live in an era of rapid change which brings with it great challenges for teachers. Our student body is becoming increasingly diverse. Teachers are working with heterogeneous groups of students, including those who may be intellectually deficient; be learning and/or physically disabled; present behavior problems; represent many different cultures; have varying degrees of English language proficiency; and/or be advanced in their knowledge. The Common Core State Standards are being implemented in almost all states and teachers are being evaluated to a large degree according to their students' performance on these standards.

At a time when fiscal crises abound, many states have allotted less funding for education. Teachers are expected to do more with less. But this need not be a great cause for concern, for with no additional monetary resources it is possible to have all students achieve academically. Success for all students can be attained to a significant degree when teachers think through their curricula more carefully and take every opportunity to apply consistently in their classrooms knowledge of how all students learn.

There is all too often a disconnect between learning theory and classroom practice. This book synthesizes and *actualizes* the main points of three main learning theories—behavioral, constructivist, and cognitive theories. Classroom applications from different grade levels and subjects show these theories in action. These applications are only a *small sampling* of a myriad of examples regarding what can be done to improve instruction. It is the intent of this author that you, when viewing these examples, will gain insights into how you can extend some of the applications within the context of your own subject and, in so doing, come up with new examples.

As you apply more of the suggestions offered in this book into your curriculum and instruction, you will notice a positive effect on your students. They will be more actively involved in learning and will experience higher academic achievement as well as personal gratification. They will enjoy your classes more, present fewer discipline problems, and provide you with greater teaching satisfaction.

Now that the Common Core State Standards (CCSS) are in effect in almost all states, it is most critical that these standards be delivered by implementing learning theory-based strategies that engage all learners. Effective implementation is integral to the success of the goal of the Common Core

State Standards—the preparation of students who are career and college ready.

Marie Menna Pagliaro

Introduction

Knowledge of learning theory is fundamental to teaching practice. The three main theories that guide classroom learning are behavioral, cognitive, and constructivist.

Behavioral theory (behaviorism) concentrates on the aspects of learning that are overtly observable and advanced by external stimuli. It is based on the stimulus-response model: Given the right stimulus, you will get the right response. The response is objective and measurable. The drill and practice model is one result of behaviorism, as is writing behavioral objectives and communicating them to students.

Cognitive theories look beyond observable behavior, viewing learning as *internal* mental processes. Students are actively involved in the way they process information (Ashcraft, 2002). Knowledge, memory, thinking, and problem solving are areas for development. Spurred by the work of Piaget (1954), knowledge is viewed as symbolic mental constructs, or schemata. When a student's schemata are changed, learning takes place. As neuroscientists continue to discover more about how the brain works, cognitive psychologists and educators are concerned with how to use that knowledge in the classroom.

The core concept in constructivism is that knowledge is *constructed* as students build new knowledge on the basis of what they have already learned. The student is *not* a passive receiver of transmitted information. Therefore, as students enter learning situations with knowledge acquired from previous experiences, their prior knowledge influences what new or modified knowledge they will build from the new learning experiences.

To build from the new experiences, learning must be active. If the new experience is inconsistent with students' present knowledge, this knowledge must be adjusted to accommodate the new experience. The constructivist teacher is curious about students' current understanding, provides experiences in which students are actively involved, allows student responses to guide subsequent lessons, promotes relevant experiential learning, and fosters self-reflection.

It is not the point of this book to argue which of these theories is best, for there is truth in all of them. Learning is a complex process that brings together cognitive, emotional, and external (environmental and social) influences and experiences that involve a student's acquiring, enhancing, or adjusting his/her knowledge, values, skills, or views of the world.

Though different learning theories involve contrasting ideas, in many cases the theories are not mutually exclusive but demonstrate overlapping or connecting ideas. For example, feedback, an important precept of behaviorism, leads to assessment, where both the student and teacher self-reflect on progress throughout the learning process and adjust accordingly, a constructivist construct. Teachers find themselves moving seamlessly through all learning theories.

To help you move comfortably through this book, chapters are divided into six main topics. Chapter 1 presents information for self-reflection at this point in your career. Knowledge of self is critical to successful classroom performance.

The second chapter describes the type of atmosphere in which any learning must be implemented (Pagliaro, 2011). This learning environment is necessary to support student participation and achievement regardless of anything else the teacher may do.

Chapters 3 through 6 incorporate within them the three basic learning theories along with numerous classroom examples. The third chapter discusses the key to all learning—motivation, what it is, and how it can be improved and sustained. The fourth chapter explains goal/objective setting and feedback, how they complement each other and establish a foundation for instruction.

Once this foundation is established, Chapter 5 analyzes the nature of the original learning (input) necessary to achieve goals and objectives, and demonstrates some critical, concrete experiences that promote the nature of the original learning so that it is encoded effectively. Finally, Chapter 6 offers some sample applications necessary to reinforce and strengthen the original learning so that it is deepened and becomes permanent.

It is important to reemphasize that in this book the chapters are not discrete subjects. There is considerable overlap among and between them. For instance, students who are motivated (Chapter 3) and are aware of goals and objectives (Chapter 4) will encode the original learning (Chapter 5) better. The original learning (Chapter 5) has to be reinforced (Chapter 6) in order to be retained.

As you read the content in each chapter, try to think of how the learning theory applications offered can be used or adapted for your particular classroom needs. The more you consciously try to apply the theories, the more adept you will become at recognizing where and how to use them with your students.

At the end of each chapter there is a self-reflection. The questions in the self-reflection themselves are designed to summarize the main points of each chapter. During this self-reflection you should try to focus not so much on what you did in the past but how you can extrapolate the classroom applications described in the text so that they can help you change and improve what you do in the future.

After the last chapter, Appendix A presents a case study that shows how one motivated teacher was able to apply learning theory to involve his entire school, his community, and eventually the nation in active learning to help solve a crisis.

Chapter One

Before You Begin

When you teach, you do so within a context. Understanding that context is critical in helping you to develop your effectiveness.

The context (environment) in which learning takes place involves numerous factors. Among them are you (the teacher), the community in which the school is located, and the students. To be a successful teacher, you should become thoroughly familiar with all of these factors. But the most control you personally have over these factors is yourself.

From the Preface you will recall that you are a very important person. *You* are the most critical part of the learning environment, the catalyst that can foster or impede learning. You should be able to capitalize on your strengths and compensate for your weaknesses. But before you can do this, you first have to know what your strengths and weaknesses are.

Socrates said, "Know thyself." Psychologists agree that it is very difficult to know ourselves for we have three faces: the social, personal, and real.

Our social face is our public image, the way we act, and how others see us. We can quickly change according to whom we want to impress. We can be "cool" in front of peers and/or try to appear intellectual to our colleagues.

Our personal face is how we perceive ourselves, the person we think we are. We can sometimes exaggerate our assets or judge ourselves too harshly.

Our real face is the true self, the reality that could be seen if we were capable of stripping away all pretense, pride, and self-deception.

SELF-DIAGNOSIS

What do you think others think of you?
What do you think of yourself?

What differences are there between how you think others see you and how you really are?

Equally important as knowing what you are is knowing what you are *not*. What are you not?

It has been said that there are three types of people—those who make things happen, those who watch things happen, and those who wonder what happened. In which of these three categories are you?

When promoting his economic issues, former Senator Phil Gramm of Texas would frequently say that there are those who push the wagon and those who ride in the wagon. What he neglected to mention was that there are those who build the wagon. Are you a wagon-builder, a wagon-pusher, or a wagon-rider?

SOME QUESTIONS FOR SELF-DIAGNOSIS

Are you risk-taker? Some people think that teachers go into the profession because they want secure jobs and are afraid to take risks. Yet risk-taking is important if you want to try new things and are willing to fail, pick up the pieces, and try again. This is the way you will grow as a teacher. Read the following to see where you stand as a risk-taker.

RISK

To laugh is to risk appearing the fool—
To weep is to risk being called sentimental—
To reach out to another is to risk involvement—
To expose feelings is to risk showing your true self—
To place your ideas and dreams before the crowd is to risk being called naïve—
To love is to risk not being loved in return—
To live is to risk dying—
To hope is to risk disappointment—
To try is to risk failure—
But risks must be taken, because the greatest risk in life is to risk nothing.
The people who risk nothing do nothing, have nothing, are nothing, and become nothing.
They may avoid suffering and sorrow, but they simply cannot learn to feel, and change, and grow, and love, and live.
Chained by their servitude, they are slaves; they forfeit their freedom.
Only the people who really risk are truly free.

—Author unknown

Well, are you a risk-taker?

Below are other questions to consider for a fuller self-understanding. As you read through them, consider how *each* might impact on your classroom performance.

What are your values? How do you really know what they are?
What are your friends' values?
Who are your heroes, the people you admire?

Attitudes determine behavior. What are your attitudes? How are they demonstrated by your behavior?

WINNING-ATTITUDE CHECK

Are you the kind of person who

- Empowers or controls?
- Wants to or has to?
- Expects success or expects failure?
- Celebrates others or complains about others?
- Learns from other people or resents others?
- Makes commitments or makes promises?
- Sees opportunities or sees problems?
- Does it or talks about it?
- Feels responsible for more than your job or cannot wait to finish your job and leave?
- Finds people doing things right or finds them doing things wrong?
- Is part of the solution or part of the problem?
- Listens or cannot wait to talk?
- Works harder than expected or is always too busy?
- Takes responsibility or finds excuses?

Are you the kind of person who says:

- "Let's find out" or "Nobody knows"
- "I'll plan to do that" or "I'll try to do that"
- "There should be a better way" or "That's the way it has always been done"
- "I was wrong" or "It wasn't my fault"
- "If it's going to happen, it's up to me" or "I cannot help it"

(Adapted from Rinke, 1997)

- What is your work ethic?
- What evidence can you give to show that you are organized?
- What do you do in your leisure time?
- What do you know about music and art?

- How do you treat people who cannot do anything for you?
- How well do you know the subject(s) you teach or are going to teach?
- What was the most recent event that caused you to change your mind?
- How enthusiastic are you about activities in which you engage?
- What evidence can you present to show that you are responsible?
- What have you done that shows you are flexible?
- How patient are you?
- Are you a good listener?
- When was the last time you admitted making a mistake?
- When was the last time you were able to show your feelings?
- Do you have a sense of humor?
- How is your self-concept?
- Do you make excuses for people, including yourself?

Tim Russert (2001), the late host of NBC's *Meet the Press*, said in a commencement address, "Indeed, there is a simple truth, 'No exercise is better for the human heart than reaching down to lift up another.'"

Does it please you to lift someone else up?
On what occasion(s) have you lifted someone else up?

Confucius has said, "Choose a job you love, and you will never have to work a day in your life."

Do you love your job?
If so, why?
If not, why?
Why did you go into teaching?
What other questions about teaching or the profession would you ask your colleagues?

SELF-REFLECTION

By reflecting honestly on the questions in this chapter, you should have identified some of your assets.

What are they?

- How will your assets contribute to your teaching?
- What weaknesses did you identify?
- How might they impede your being effective in the classroom?
- What will you *do* with the results of your self-reflection?

Chapter Two

Setting the Tone for Learning in Your 21st Century Classroom

There is no doubt that our society is changing rapidly. Information continues to double every 72 hours and will be exploding even more quickly in the future (Jensen, 1998). Our classrooms are increasing in social, emotional, cultural, and academic diversity. Moreover, classrooms are more inclusive and heterogeneous.

In this new society, people will be changing jobs approximately every five years. The demands of these new jobs will require skills associated with team membership; listening; self-management; time management; assuming responsibility; and following schedules (Secretary's Commission on Achieving Necessary Skills, 1991).

There is a strong relationship between the needs of the workforce and classroom teaching (Goleman, 1998). Goleman's research found that *lack of self-control* is a primary factor for lack of success in the workforce, with a sense of helplessness and frequent distractions as the most important reasons for poor job performance. In contrast, high job performance occurs when there are high expectations of employees who are allowed to set their own goals for achieving these expectations, and when the employees receive prompt feedback and exhibit good listening skills (Cummings, 2000).

States are currently attempting to revamp education to meet the demands of the 21st century by including life skills, a wide range of intellectual skills, and social skills. There is agreement between leaders in both industry and academia that students have to learn to become innovative, solve problems, and interact successfully with people from many different cultures (Gewertz, 2008).

Curriculum and instruction have to reflect the needs of the 21st century. This means that students must be involved meaningfully in learning, because if they are not, they will find their own ways to become engaged, often to the detriment of themselves, to the rest of the class, and eventually, to society.

Students should be invited to add their own curriculum goals in addition to those of the teacher; be given choices regarding how they will learn; self-reflect and monitor their goal achievement; redirect their effort, when necessary; and play an essential role in their own assessment/evaluation (Kolis & Krusack, 2012). It is noteworthy that attention to the development of student independence has been lacking in teacher education programs (Kaufman & Moss, 2010).

Students should be involved in relevant experiences, authentic problems, and when age appropriate, should participate in constructing scoring rubrics. Depending on the situation, students may work independently or in groups, check each other's work, coach when warranted, with all individual members taking responsibility for the group's achievements and supporting each other to attain success.

When implementing an effective curriculum, the teacher relies less on lectures and sequential lessons than on active, project-based, hands-on learning. In this environment students learn skills and concepts entrenched in these activities which are accompanied by fluid time frames. The teacher uses primary sources, inside as well as outside resources, and electronics as opposed to the textbook or worksheets as predominant means of instruction.

Wolk (2008) suggests that we introduce "joy" in learning. Some ways this may be accomplished is by giving students choices; allowing students to create things; reading good books; having some fun together; showing off students' work; and providing them time to tinker.

For any instruction based on learning theory to be most effective, that instruction must be implemented in a supportive, tension-free learning environment. In this positive environment the teacher is a facilitator who fosters not only students' academic growth but also their personal and social growth.

The positive classroom is a learning community in which there is shared responsibility for the success of all community members. There is a warm, friendly atmosphere where all members show mutual respect for and support each other in a spirit of cooperation in which all have a stake in the success of all other members. This atmosphere produces a *comfort level* in which students are more willing to take risks and participate in learning activities that advance achievement.

"Positive relationships between teachers and students are among the most commonly cited variables associated with effective instruction. If the relationship is strong, instructional strategies seem to be more effective. Conversely, a weak or negative relationship will mute or even negate the benefits of even the most effective instructional strategies" (Marzano, 2011, p. 82).

Mendler (2013) suggests that teachers can begin to create a positive classroom and school climate by seeking feedback on themselves. "Give your students a class assignment to write at least two specific things about you that they like the most and that help them be successful. You can also have your students do this with each other to help improve the classroom climate." He goes on to suggest that teachers ask parents to communicate one positive thing they have observed or heard about your class from their child and that teachers invite colleagues to observe classes to get input regarding what was done well and what could be done better.

While in the past teachers were taught to control student behavior, now teachers are focusing on developing strategies that support students' making good choices (McLeod, Fisher, & Hoover, 2003). Teachers and students listen carefully to each other. Feedback is prompt on the part of both. There is a sharing of leadership between teachers and students as the teacher no longer controls but fosters student self-control and responsibility.

The teacher's role is one of a guide and coach as opposed to pouring information and rules into students' heads. The teacher determines rules collaboratively with students and there is shared responsibility for implementing and enforcing rules. This sharing is particularly important because "a sense of efficacy, control, or self-determination is critical if people are to feel intrinsically motivated. When people come to believe that the events and outcomes in their lives are mostly uncontrollable, they have developed learned helplessness" (Woolfolk, 2008, p. 371).

Several characteristics have been demonstrated to be conducive to promoting a positive emotional classroom environment: having a caring attitude, setting high standards, and having *all* classroom members, including the teacher, show mutual respect and support for each other (Oakes & Lipton, 2003). In short, there is a sense of community in the class where all classroom members are connected with one another. "How students feel in your classroom influences how they perform in your classroom" (Ginsburg, 2012).

In her first teaching experience, Meier (2012) was shocked by how "a disrespectful setting hurts kids—leading us to miss some children's potential for curiosity, thoughtfulness, creativity, independent spirit, and their relentless love of learning."

The foundation of student respect is based on the premise that "you and the class care enough about each other to make sure they behave in a manner that is in their best interest and the best interest of others" (Canter, 2006, p. 26). But you should also note that students like teachers who are trusting and caring and who treat students with respect. When students believe that teachers care for and value them, the students are more cooperative in complying with teachers' requests. These teachers have more influence on students than teachers not so perceived (Jones & Jones, 2003).

Caring teachers→→→Student appreciation→→→Student cooperation

Research has indicated that rapport with the teacher and fellow classmates made students feel connected and willing to participate, thus enhancing cognitive and affective learning (Frisby & Martin, 2010). This supportive learning environment welcomes student questions; is nonjudgmental; fosters the attitude that it is all right to make mistakes because we all do and learn from them; and does not allow students to be subjected to ridicule from anyone in the learning community. Students are given the time to think and are challenged at their appropriate levels.

In this supportive classroom the teacher might say, "We are in this together. When one of us succeeds, we all succeed. When one of us fails, we all fail. It is critically important to me personally that all of us do well." This is a very powerful message, but it remains powerful only *if it is implemented consistently.*

Annette Breaux, an internationally renowned author and speaker, added her voice to a blog by Larry Ferlazzo (2012).

> If your first (and daily) impression on your students is not a positive one, you're doomed to a miserable school year, and so are your students. The fact is that students need (and deserve) to be surrounded by positive adults. No student can possibly benefit from having another negative adult in his life. And none of us can ever have enough positive role models in our lives. So why is it that there are teachers in classrooms who do not appear happy? And how do you think it would feel, as a student, to spend an entire school year in the classroom of someone who appears unhappy and serious most of the time? This is not to suggest that when a student behaves inappropriately, you should appear happy about it. Use your common sense in this situation. The most effective teachers know how to appear serious while remaining calm and professional, but never personally offended. This is also not to suggest that if you appear happy, you'll be a great teacher. BUT, all great teachers do have positive demeanors, so it's a vital ingredient to success in the classroom.

Engel & Sandstrom (2010) have concluded from their research that our students lack a sense of responsibility for each other's welfare. To address this void they recommend that schools "teach children how to be good to one another, how to cooperate, how to defend someone who is being picked on and how to stand up for what is right" (p. A2).

Brooks (2011) has described the successful classroom as engaging and well managed. In this classroom there is a strong interrelationship between student and teacher in an atmosphere of trust in which students feel free to participate. When trusting, respectful, caring relationships exist between students and teachers, the students will become engaged learners and thrive.

Kohn (1996) makes the point that students do not become more likely to think for themselves or care about others when teachers take all responsibility for rules and expectations for student behavior and consequences for noncompliance. He encourages teachers to assist students in becoming compassionate, in assuming responsibility, and in being reflective by taking the unpredictable and likely messy route which involves having the students work together in deciding how to be fair and in determining what respect means.

Successful contemporary teachers have students participate in establishing **rules** and **procedures** (Marzano, 2003, 2007; Curwin, Mendler, & Mendler, 2008), and *do so at the very beginning of school.* A rule conveys a general expectation that can be applied in many different circumstances, such as, "Listen when others are speaking"; a procedure states a course of action for a routine such as a method for passing out or collecting materials. Rules/procedures should be reasonable, clear, short, explained, practiced when applicable, displayed, and minimal with approximately five for elementary school students (Emmer, Evertson, & Worsham, 2003a) and around seven for middle/secondary (Emmer, Evertson, & Worsham, 2003b).

There is a difference between behavior and classroom management. Behavior is related to discipline, and classroom management has to do with procedures and routines. According to Wong and Wong (2005), teachers who are ineffective discipline students with consequences and punishments whereby teachers who are effective manage their classrooms with procedures, rules, and routines.

Taking time to explain rules and procedures is highly recommended because in order to be implemented, they must be understood (Good & Brophy, 2003). It is also effective to explain the reasons *why* the rules are important. This practice is especially important for students whose cultures may not be compatible with rules and procedures normally implemented in American classrooms.

Rules should be *reasonable*. There are four criteria for reasonable rules and procedures. They must be necessary, capable of being performed by the students, not run against human nature, and not require for their enforcement more resources than you can afford (McLeod, Fisher, & Hoover, 2003). When establishing rules, the teacher should concentrate not only on what to do with students who do not comply with the rules, but more important on what these students are being asked to do (Kohn, 1996).

As a contemporary teacher who is aware of feedback provided by students, show that you are aware of and sensitive to students' feelings. Try to pick up on attitudes that may come across in artwork, written work, or during discussions. *You teach students how to treat you and each other by the way you treat them.* If you show respect for, and are courteous and sensitive to all students, they will tend to model your behavior back toward you and toward each other.

Make sure that all students are active participants in *meaningful* activities. Prepare a sociogram for each class. Identify who are the **isolates**, the students selected by no one or very few classmates as those with whom they would like to work, and the **stars**, the students picked by many classmates as those with whom they would like to work. Attempt to pair or group the isolates into instructional activities with more socially accepted students so that all will feel welcome in the class. Isolates will be more welcomed by socially accepted students if you have at the beginning of school established and then continuously reinforced a supportive classroom environment.

In recent school shootings, one common factor regarding the perpetrators was that they were loners. Some reasons for feeling that they were loners could be explained by a popular song that begins with the following words: "You're nobody till somebody loves you. You're nobody till somebody cares." In a successful learning community everyone should feel as though he or she is *somebody* and that all class members, especially the teacher, are bonded with and care about him or her. Bonding is especially critical for middle and high school students.

> Being liked by teachers can offset the effects of peer rejection in middle school. And, students who have few friends, but are not rejected—simply ignored by other students—can remain well-adjusted academically and socially when they are liked and supported by teachers. (Woolfolk, 2008, p. 453)

As a shared leader, never lose sight of the fact that you are a role model, a *critical* role model for your students. Behave like a mature person they can look up to by using proper speech, grammar, and by dressing professionally. While clothes may not make a person, they can be major factors in ***un***making a person (Wong & Wong, 1998).

Research reveals that the clothing worn by teachers affects the work, attitude, and discipline of students. You dress for four main effects:

1. Respect
2. Credibility
3. Acceptance
4. Authority (p. 55)

Teachers often complain that they do not get the respect awarded other professions. Their colleagues retort that those teachers may not be well groomed, may even speak and behave like the students, making it difficult for *all* teachers to gain public and student respect.

Some do's and don'ts when using language in the classroom were recommended by Ryan, Cooper, and Tauer (2008) (See Table 2.1).

Establish a positive but realistic level of expectation not only for academics but also for behavior. When working with the students to establish rules and procedures, convey the attitude that you know your students can learn subject matter and behave properly, and *do not give up on any student*. The confidence you exhibit will often give students the extra incentive they may need. Many successful people can trace their success, or possibly their redirection in life, to the fact that one person, usually a teacher, believed in them and encouraged them, especially with the support of the class. *You* have the potential to be that person.

As a 21st century teacher, be responsive to students' reactions and feedback by constantly assessing and changing immediately, with the suggestions of the students, whatever instruction or method of dealing with improper behavior is not working. Model flexibility by trying out new teaching strategies, new materials, or new activities. If you are not particularly creative or innovative, you can still be resourceful.

In a successful learning community a teacher wants to promote a cooperative spirit through shared leadership and developing student self-control. Show that you are aware of the fact that "control over one's life is something that everyone wants and needs. When we don't get it, we go after control over others. Because many of our discipline problems in school either start or end with a power struggle, it is a good idea to look at the idea of sharing control with the students" (McLeod, Fisher, & Hoover, 2003, p. 66).

Interact with your students in a friendly (not overfriendly) but businesslike manner. "A businesslike classroom refers to a learning environment in which the students and the teacher conduct themselves in ways suggesting that achieving specified learning goals takes priority over other concerns" (Cangelosi, 2008, p. 58). Remember that you do not have to be loved by your students; you have to be respected. Students do not like or respect teachers who let them get away with misbehavior.

Interacting positively with students makes teaching less stressful, with students enjoying your classes more. Once you have established this suppor-

Table 2.1. PROFESSIONAL CLASSROOM SPEECH

DO'S	DON'TS
Speak clearly and concisely	Use filler words such as "uh," "like," "you know"
Use gender-neutral terms	Address students as "Guys," "You guys" or "Fellows"; Say instead, "Class" or "Boys and Girls"
Use proper grammar	Use expletives or profanity

(Adapted from Ryan, Cooper, & Tauer, 2008, p.75)

tive learning environment with your students, you will be well on your way to implementing learning theory more effectively.

In conclusion, Michael Anderson, a math teacher who had a disastrous first year, and eventually became his district's Teacher of the Year, came up with his recipe for a successful classroom. "Earn students' respect, create an environment where it's safe for them to try and even fail, and then make the material relevant to their lives" (Gammill, 2010).

ATTRIBUTES OF A POSITIVE 21ST CENTURY CLASSROOM
Student centered
Shared control by all class members
Student participation in making, implementing, and enforcing rules
Constant feedback from teacher to students, from students to teacher, and from student to student
Increase in student responsibility
Teacher helps student make good choices
Teacher fosters student self-control
Careful listening among all class members, including the teacher
Classroom atmosphere warm, friendly, and caring
All class members have mutual respect for and support each other in a spirit of cooperation
All have a stake in the success of all other members
All class members are bonded with each other

SCENARIO: TRADITIONAL CLASSROOM

Mr. Jack Watson has been teaching a fifth-grade class for the last four years. He teaches in a culturally diverse community, and his classroom reflects that diversity. As his class enters the room at the beginning of the school year, Mr. Watson is writing their homework assignment on the board. His list of usual class rules is already displayed on a poster in a highly visible place. Many of the students are somewhat chatty as they come into the class, but they finally settle down, most sitting toward the back of the room. Mr. Watson takes the attendance. He prints his name on the board and begins class by telling the students, quite excitedly, what they are going to learn this year. He makes a point of telling them also how he will conduct instruction, and how they will be assessed so that they will know how well they are progressing. Before beginning his lesson, Mr. Watson points to the rules that class must follow and discusses each of them, why they are important, and what will happen when the students do not follow the rules.

21ST CENTURY CLASSROOM: TRANSFORMATION 1

After reading Chapter 2 of this book, Mr. Watson realizes that much of his approach has not been consistent with the 21st century needs of his students. Though he had some sense of the way the society was moving, he had been unaware that students would need to be more active team members, assume more responsibility, be good listeners, solve problems, and interact successfully with different cultures, not only within the community but throughout the world.

He would have to be more flexible by allowing students to set their own goals in addition to his, offer more choices in the way they learn, and have more control over their assessments. Even though he believed that he presented his material with enthusiasm, he concluded that he would need to offer more authentic experiences, projects, and group work.

Most important, Mr. Watson understands that he has to let go of control not only of the curriculum and instruction but also of the management of the classroom. While these were areas where he would ultimately have to be responsible, he had to share control and responsibility with his students. He slowly began to make this change this academic year. But next year his first lesson would be establishing rules and procedures, giving his students the authority to enforce these rules and procedures, including consequences for not following them.

Though he always showed respect for his students, he wanted to reinforce the need for their showing respect for each other. He was determined to have a caring classroom where everyone had a stake in the success of all other members by supporting each other.

Mr. Watson found the challenge of setting up this type of classroom exciting. Also, he knew that if he was going to succeed, he would have to discuss his new way of looking at curriculum, instruction, and classroom management with the administration and other faculty members. Just as students in his class needed to support each other, members of the administration and faculty had to support each other, too.

21ST CENTURY CLASSROOM: TRANSFORMATION 2

Mr. Watson was pleased that he didn't have to change everything he was doing. But he did want to make some adjustments. The next time his students entered the room at the beginning of school, instead of putting the homework on the board, he asked them to write on the topic "What Are the Most Important Things That You Should Know about Me?" to include what they were good at and enjoyed and what they would like to accomplish. He was determined to incorporate this information into his lessons. While his students were involved in this activity, he took the attendance. He made a special point of learning their names quickly so that he could call them by name during the next activity.

He introduced himself to the class while pointing to his name on the board. He told them how long he was teaching, where he went to school, and the fact that he was married with two children.

Together, he and the students immediately established the rules and procedures, including the consequences for not following them. Periodically, he checked with the class to see how the rules and procedures were working and if the students had any suggestions for modifying them. Mr. Watson was pleased that he showed respect for his students. They seemed to have picked up on this message and began to show more respect for each other. He video recorded his class to note his speech and grammar. He was satisfied that he always dressed professionally, noting how some teachers in his school were not, and how diminished they were in their students' eyes.

SELF-REFLECTION

- What input do your students have in making rules and procedures?
- What evidence is there that you respect your students and that they respect each other?
- How do your students support each other?
- What input do your students have in making curriculum and assessment decisions?
- How meaningful are the activities you offer your students?
- What choices do you offer them?
- How do you foster your students' personal and social growth?
- How safe do your students feel to take risks in your class?
- How well do all your students participate in class?
- How professional is your dress, your speech?

Chapter Three

Securing and Maintaining Student Motivation

Motivation is a psychological state that stimulates, directs, and sustains behavior. Most psychologists believe that motivation is the key to all learning, for a motivated person learns better and faster, and will overcome many obstacles to achieve a goal. The more a person desires to learn, the greater the probability that s/he will.

Motivation can lead to several positive results on student learning, including how students connect with subject matter. Motivation can lead behavior toward certain goals; increase effort; increase initiation of activities; improve persistence; develop cognitive functioning; and generally lead to performance improvement. In short, motivation is the mother's milk of learning.

INTRINSIC AND EXTRINSIC MOTIVATION

There are basically two types of motivation: intrinsic and extrinsic. Intrinsic motivation is the inner desire or natural tendency to do something. It is performing an activity for the sake of the activity, especially when the activity is not required. Intrinsic motivation is self-sustaining (Deci & Ryan, 1985).

Extrinsic motivation is that which comes from outside factors such as incentives (rewards) or punishments. The reward is not in performing the task itself but in the what's-in-it-for-me attitude. A task is performed because a reward will result for task completion, or punishment for noncompletion.

Though many students come to school with the inner desire to learn (the ideal), the reality is that many others do not. It is then incumbent upon the teacher to create the motivation that supports learning by capturing and maintaining students' interest (Brophy, 1988).

ANTICIPATORY SET

Interest can be aroused by using an *anticipatory set*, also known as set induction. The purpose of the set is to provide a hook to gain the students' attention, raise their curiosity, and connect them with new instruction.

The set can often be used to introduce some cognitive dissonance, incompatible ideas that are simultaneously held. This lack of "fit" in the psyche causes psychological discomfort, a little frustration (stress, tension, uneasiness) which throws students off balance just enough to make them want to come back into a state of equilibrium. And this coming back into equilibrium is the process where learning takes place.

The science of teaching tells the teacher that the right amount of frustration should be introduced. The art of teaching determines how much frustration is just right. Too little frustration leads to boredom; too much frustration turns students off. Initiating frustration is like giving someone a vaccine. If too much of the dead or weakened agent is injected, a patient could become seriously ill by possibly actually developing the disease. If the amount of dead or weakened agent is too little, the vaccine will probably not immunize the patient. But if just the right amount is injected, the patient will become resistant to the disease.

Classroom application 3.1

> Mr. Jacobs: How many of you brought your lunch to school?
>
> [All hands go up.] What did you bring, Tom?
>
> Tom: Peanut butter and jelly.
>
> Mr. Jacobs: [Pats his belly.] One of my favorites. What about you, Henrietta?
>
> Henrietta: A tuna fish sandwich.
>
> [Some members of the class hold their noses, snicker, or say, "Yuk." Mr. Jacobs ignores the behavior.]
>
> Mr. Jacobs: Tuna is a very good source of protein, Henrietta. Whoever prepared that lunch is smart and must really care about you. And what do you have for lunch, George?

George: A ham sandwich.

Mr. Jacobs: Also a great source of protein. Well, class, I brought my lunch today, too. [Mr. Jacobs places his lunch box on the desk.] What do you think is in my lunch box? Frank.

Frank: Soup and crackers.

Mr. Jacobs: Maybe. What do you think, Johnny?

Johnny: A Big Mac.

Mr. Jacobs: It's possible. And you, Sheila?

Sheila: Chicken nuggets . . . or a hot dog. But, but then, by lunchtime, the hot dog would be cold. [The class laughs.]

Mr. Jacobs: Good guesses, but in my lunch box is *another* lunch box.

[The students all look at each other with puzzled faces (discomfort level), obviously having been thrown off balance. Mr. Jacobs opens his lunch box. The students look with anticipation. In the lunch box is a lima bean. Mr. Jacobs places the lima bean on his desk.]

Mr. Jacobs: So what do you think we are going to learn today? [There is a long pause as the teacher observes the still crinkled faces.] Debbie.

Debbie: How . . . how or why a lima bean is a lunch box?

Mr. Jacobs: Excellent, Debbie, now who can say that another way? Jerry.

Jerry: How a lunch box and a lima bean are the same.

Mr. Jacobs: Great, Jerry. Give us another way of saying this. Paul.

Paul: What makes a lima bean like lunch.

Note that in the example the teacher did not tell the students at the beginning what the objective of the lesson was. *The objective flowed from the anticipatory set*—what the teacher did to stimulate curiosity so that the students would want to know the objective—how the lunch box and lima bean were alike.

Some teachers just state the objective at the beginning. For example, a teacher might say, "Today we're going to learn about a lima bean" or, given a different lesson, "Today we are going to learn how sounds are produced."

Merely stating the purpose of the lesson is *much less efficient* than throwing the students a little off balance in the beginning with the anticipatory set and letting the objective derive from that set.

Classroom application 3.2

> Mr. Frederic: Raise your hand if you think we are closer to the sun in the summer. [Almost all hands go up. Mr. Frederic is aware that this is a common misconception even among adults. He then displays a model of the Earth's orbit around the sun with the seasons labeled. He gives the students some time to observe the model.]
>
> Mr. Frederic: Raise your hand if you still think the Earth is closer to the sun in the summer. [No hands go up.] You have observed well because we are actually farther from the sun in the summer, and today we are going to learn why we are actually warmer in summer even though we are farther from the sun.

The students then proceed to examine the sun, earth, and its orbit to hypothesize what factors exist that could possibly influence the warmth of the earth during the summer even though they observe in the model that the earth's distance is farther from the sun.

Another type of set induction that can be used to motivate students is introducing a problem whose solution is made possible only by the achievement of the lesson objective. In this type of situation, the learning becomes more meaningful because there is a *reason* to learn something (Hunter, 2004).

Classroom application 3.3

> Ms. Pauley: Mrs. Sheridan just informed me that our class mothers raised $476 from our bake sale to buy a carpet for our classroom. But before we can buy that carpet, we first have to decide how much we need to cover the floor. And to do this we have to learn how to measure area. [Unless the students can measure area (solve the problem by achieving the lesson objective), the class cannot buy the carpet (the reason for the learning)].

It should be noted that time spent on the anticipatory set (set induction) should be relatively short, leaving the largest portion of lesson time to accomplishing the lesson objective.

ATTENTION

Neuroscientists have concluded that the only way we know that learning has taken place is through memory, and the only way we can get to memory is through *attention*. As has already been stated, motivation is critical to gaining and maintaining students' attention.

The brain is always paying attention to something. Our survival depends on it (Jensen, 1998). When teachers say that a student is not paying attention, what they really mean is that the student is paying attention to something but not to the lesson. Though students can process information peripherally without direct attention (Caine & Caine, 1994), this type of processing does not lead to higher levels of understanding.

The student's attention can be gained through the *emotions*. The emotions are powerful attention getters. The best way to reach a student emotionally is by making the learning *personal*. How can you capitalize on students' personal interests? How can you make learning personal to them, their families, or to their neighborhoods? It must be made clear to students what the content means to them personally and how it can be applied.

$$\text{Emotions} \rightarrow \rightarrow \rightarrow \text{Attention} \rightarrow \rightarrow \rightarrow \text{Memory}$$

How often have you been in two or three classes with the same instructor who still did not know your name? How connected and involved did that make you feel?

Nothing is more personal to a student than his or her name. Effective teachers are aware of the importance of making instruction more personal by getting to know their students by name right away and immediately *calling them by name*.

Effective teachers make it a point to learn something personal about each student and *use* this information in instruction. When students are involved personally, they become more involved emotionally. And "emotions . . . are not the cards at the game table but the table itself" (Jensen, 2005, p. 80). Learning students' names and positive information about them quickly may be more difficult in departmentalized classes, prevalent in middle/high schools, where teachers can be assigned 125 students or more. Still, make a concerted effort to know each student, *and the sooner the better*.

Classroom application 3.4

Ms. Goldberg decided to plan an activity to have all her students get to know each other by name, and then address each other by name during class. She distributed 5x8 cards to all her fifth graders and asked them to write a symbol or word that best described them. Then, each student in turn stated his or her name, what the rest of the students should know about him or her, and explained what the symbol or word communicated.

After this activity, Ms. Goldberg immediately began her lesson, calling each student by name, practicing and enforcing the students' addressing each other by name. Her students continued to address each other by name consistently throughout the academic year.

Learning can also be made personal by using the names of students in the class during the lesson such as in math problems or in stories.

Classroom application 3.5

> Ms. Vargas: Luis had 12 apples. He wanted to share them equally with Carmen, Helen, and Juan. [Luis, Carmen, Helen, and Juan are all class members.] How many apples did he give each of them? Remember that Luis wants his apples, too. [Students then manipulate objects representing apples or apples themselves to determine the answer.]
>
> Ms. Vargas: How many groups shared apples? [Pause] Luis.
>
> Luis: Four.
>
> Ms. Vargas: Great. Now how many apples did each member of the group get? [Pause] Carmen.
>
> Carmen: Three.
>
> Ms. Vargas: So, Carmen, if we divide 12 apples into four groups, how many will be in each group?
>
> Carmen: Three.
>
> Ms. Vargas: Can you turn that into a number sentence?
>
> Carmen: 12 divided by 4 equals 3.

There are available e-books that have the recipient's name inserted as the hero, and names of his or her friends or relatives as characters. What person would not want to read a story about himself and about those whom he know? The teacher can include the names of class members in the e-books to make them more personal.

Attention can also be solicited by priming the brain. This means that students will note something if *their attention is directed to it*.

Classroom application 3.6

> Mr. Simpson: Today you are going to find out how to begin to use the Internet for research.

Classroom application 3.7

> Ms. Johnson: In the video, note *in particular* how the blood flows through the heart.

Classroom application 3.8

> Ms. Spector: When we read this story, I want you to pay particular attention to who the main characters are, what they are doing to make life difficult for Mrs. Warren, and how she handles their behavior.

Keeping learning personal means finding out about students' cultures. In the culturally diverse 21st century classroom, be genuinely curious about different cultures represented by your students. However, always remember that each individual in any cultural group may not conform to the cultural norm. Social scientists will confirm that there are greater differences between individuals *within* a group than there are *between* groups. The prior sentence is so important that you should repeat it to yourself in **different** words.

Ask students to share their customs with you and capitalize on these customs during instruction.

Classroom application 3.9

A few weeks before school began, Ms. Lennon checked the backgrounds of the students who were going to be in her classroom. She found that there were 7 African Americans, 8 Latinos, 4 Asian Americans, 3 Native Americans, and 3 Caucasians. In previous years she had had African American and Latino students. She was sure that she had accumulated the following information for both groups: food; religion; economics; politics; family structure and values; ways of communicating; general attitudes and beliefs; group norms; traditions/history; mental processing and learning styles; dress and appearance; rewards and recognition; social interaction; group v. individual needs; music; sense of self and space; time consciousness; and attitude toward work.

This was the first time that she would have Native Americans and Asian Americans, so she studied the same information for those groups. A Caucasian herself, she did not feel the need to learn more about this group.

On the first day of school, Ms. Lennon wanted to ensure that her classroom encouraged cultural respect and sensitivity. She greeted them with a "hello" in each language from her students' cultures. She communicated to her students a sense of common purpose in which all were expected to respect and support each other.

Already displayed around the room were books that represented people with different skin colors and pictures of children with different features, hair colors, styles, and textures. For future display she collected pictures of people with different skin colors depicted in positive terms and in many different occupations. She was already anticipating how she could use the music and holidays of her students' cultures.

Ms. Lennon reviewed the Common Core curriculum for her grade, and with the guidance of the librarian, selected at the appropriate level of complexity several corresponding texts that represented literature and heroes from cultures of her students.

As the days progressed, she asked her students how they expressed common terms in their languages. Then she posted these terms on the bulletin board.

During instruction, Ms. Lennon focused on using heterogeneous small-group instruction.

Attention can be gained through experiences to which students can relate. These experiences are more motivational.

Classroom application 3.10

> Mr. Scott: Boys and girls, how many of you have ever gone to a grocery store or supermarket? [All hands go up.]
>
> Mr. Scott: That's great, what did you buy?

[Students begin to name what they bought. Whenever a liquid is mentioned, Mr. Scott lists it on the board.]

> Mr. Scott: [Points to list.] How are all these items that you bought the same? George.
>
> George: [Waits for a while.] They're all liquids.
>
> Mr. Scott: That's right, George. [Teacher writes the title "Liquids" above the list.] And because you have all bought liquids, it is important for you to know how to measure liquids. So what are we going to learn today? Marilyn.
>
> Marilyn: How to measure liquids.

Mr. Scott: And, Marilyn, why is it important that we know how to measure liquids?

Marilyn: Because we've all bought them.

Mr. Scott: Thank you, Marilyn. And in particular all of you should know how some of the measures we use—cups, pints, and quarts—are related to each other, and since they're sometime written on the containers as abbreviations, and we're studying abbreviations in language arts, we'll identify those abbreviations also. [Mr. Scott writes on the board, Objective: To determine how cups, pints, and quarts are related and to state their abbreviations.] I want several of you to restate the objective in your own words. Pedro.

Pedro: How are liquids measured?

Mr. Scott: Excellent, Pedro, but be more specific.

Pedro: How are cups, pints, and quarts measured?

Mr. Scott: Good, Pedro, now who can tell us our objective in another way? Inez.

Inez: We're going to find out how to measure liquids we buy, especially cups, pints, and quarts, and find out what their abbreviations are.

Mr. Scott: And why is knowing that important for *you* [personal] to know? Henry.

Henry: Because I bought them and use them.

Personal motivation can be enhanced by using the pronoun "you" in lessons and in classroom interactions. Note that in the previous classroom application, 3.10, Mr. Scott emphasized the importance of the content for "you" to know.

Note also how "you" can be used effectively by teachers in demonstrating sensitivity and support by communicating that they have heard and understand students' feelings by paraphrasing some of their comments made in frustration or anger.

Classroom application 3.11

Tyrone: I hate chemistry.

Ms. Young: *You*'re having difficulty balancing this equation [paraphrase]. Let's see if we can work with each other to make it easier for *you* to balance it.

Many teachers keep learning personal by showing that they are interested in their students as people.

Classroom application 3.12

Mr. Donato has a personal chat with each of his students. In particular he wants to find out more about that student and what *together* he can do to make the student successful.

"When teachers consciously had personal conversations with students for more than two minutes at a time over 10 days . . . they saw an 85% improvement in classroom management for that student" (Franklin, 2006, p. 5). He uses the analogy of a cramped muscle in dealing with students, especially the most behavior challenged. Students desire a positive personal connection with an adult authority figure, and when they get that positive connection, the muscle relaxes over time leaving the students free to concentrate on learning (Franklin, 2006).

Motivation is improved when the teacher acknowledges the personal/positive in each student. Comments such as those offered by the following two teachers go a long way in keeping them and their students connected.

Classroom application 3.13

    Mr. Olinsky: Wow, Jamal, that's a sharp shirt.

Classoom application 3.14

    Ms. Schwartz: Kevin, you've shown great improvement in your computation skills.

[When a student accomplishes a challenging task for their performance level, Ms. Schwartz finds it worth her while to apply what she learned by reading Marzano (2007). She recognizes these achievements by communicating with the home through calling, sending an e-mail, a note, or a certificate of accomplishment.]

All students appreciate the personal attention of teachers. For some students the need for the teacher to show some personal interest in them is paramount to and has a positive impact on their learning.

Classroom application 3.15

Mr. Clark makes it a point to talk with students informally before, during, and after class about their interests.

Classroom application 3.16

Ms. Harper greets students outside of school at extracurricular events or at stores.

Classroom application 3.17

Mr. Jackson singles out a few students each day in the lunchroom and strikes up a conversation with them.

Classroom application 3.18

Ms. Benedict goes out of her way to be aware of and comment on important events in students' lives such as participation in sports, drama, or other extracurricular activities. She then compliments students on important achievements in and outside of school.

Classroom application 3.19

Mr. Paige meets his students at the door as they come into the class every day and says hello to each student, making sure to use their first name.

Teachers can keep learning personal (and emotional) by displaying pictures of the students doing work or involved in special projects.

Classroom application 3.20

Mr. Campbell keeps the motivation momentum going by taking pictures of his students engaged in productive activities. He displays the pictures on a bulletin board with a corresponding title. Some titles he has used are: "Look at What We Have Learned," "When We Work Hard, We Succeed," and "We Like to Be Challenged." Mr. Campbell knows that hard work gives his students a feeling of accomplishment. And accomplishment itself becomes self-motivating.

He makes every student feel important by arranging some work the student can display or present. Periodically, Mr. Campbell video records students working on meaningful projects or students not working productively. He shows the video and has the students provide input regarding how *their* work habits were successful, or how productivity can be improved.

Whenever the occasion allows, offer students the opportunity to talk about themselves. "People like to talk about themselves and the things that interest them" (Marzano, 2007, p. 114). Providing this activity allows students to remain emotionally and personally involved in learning, especially when you connect what you know about them personally or their interests to the knowledge and skills to be studied, as Mr. Campbell did in classroom application 3.20.

INFORMATION ON KNOWLEDGE GAIN

Covington (1992) discovered that students, especially those who operate on avoiding failure and competition, are highly motivated by being informed of their *knowledge gain*. This positive report on their progress, even if small, leads students to want to learn further.

Classroom application 3.21

> Ms. Kendall: Jack, I was just looking at your paper. Last time you had four errors in grammar and now you have just one. That is real progress. You should be very proud of yourself. Let's check that one error so that the next time you won't have any.

CHOICE

It is also now recognized that one of the most potent student motivators is *choice* (Erwin, 2004). Teachers who place a high priority on allowing students to choose their methods of instruction, assessments, and eventual evaluation communicate a trust in the students to make the best choices for themselves, producing learners who become intrinsically motivated to succeed. Depending on student age/maturity level, the choices can be creating a smartphone app, developing a marketing plan for a business within the community, designing a suit for astronauts to wear on another planet, or building a city capable of generating its own electricity (Waidelich, 2012).

Choice gives students "the opportunity to embrace their own learning by giving them the chance to find out what they care about or take an interest in. In great classrooms with innovative educators, this is done every day while meeting standards and raising test scores" (Waidelich, 2012).

Classroom application 3.22

Mr. Paley has completed a lesson on pronouns. He offers his students the choice of working on a computer program, a pronoun puzzle, constructing their own pronoun graphic, or completing a workbook to reinforce their knowledge of pronouns.

Classroom application 3.23

Mr. Williams engages his eighth graders at the end of a unit on community development. He allows them to choose their method of assessment by selecting the opportunity to create a smartphone app; give a presentation to the city council; develop a marketing plan for a pet store in the community that is in danger of closing; adjust the energy use of the community to make it more energy independent and efficient; develop a brochure to attract tourists to the community; or suggest their own meaningful and relevant assessments.

EXPLOITING ONE'S PASSION

Csikszentmihalyi (1990) reported that when students are passionate about something, they will be motivated enough to overcome obstacles to achieve. For a vast majority of students there is at least one subject, topic, or activity that excites and, therefore, motivates them. Identifying this passion and capitalizing on it during learning will lead to that student's progress. It is incumbent upon teachers to find out what students are passionate about or what they really enjoy.

Classroom application 3.24

Mr. Stafford has been working with Darren to improve his math skills. By chatting with Darren, Mr. Stafford found out that Darren loves baseball. When it was time for the class to learn how to compute averages, Mr. Stafford had Darren learn how to compute baseball averages and then teach this computation to the rest of the class. Mr. Stafford found several books about baseball for Darren to read as well as articles about Darren's favorite players.

TEACHER EXPECTATIONS

Teachers' *expectations* have a strong influence on students. According to a research review conducted by the Education Commission of the States reported by Heitin (2013), "Teachers' expectations—often influenced by factors such as race, ethnicity, and family income levels—can significantly affect students' academic performance. Negative teacher expectations account for an estimated 5 to10 percent of the variance in student achievement and contribute to achievement gaps between white and minority students."

Teachers who communicate a positive level of expectation motivate *all* students to perform. Examine the attitudes conveyed by the following teachers:

Classroom application 3.25

> Ms. Giganti: This problem will be a little challenging, but I know you can do it.

Classroom application 3.26

> Mr. Lee: You did this type of problem so well the last time, I am sure that you can do another that's just a little more difficult.

Classroom application 3.27

> Ms. Loeffer: Try working on these questions about the novel. I know that you will answer them thoughtfully because you enjoyed the novel so much. If you have any difficulty, which I don't expect, I am here for you.

SUCCESS

An old adage states, "Nothing succeeds like success." Motivation can be increased by having students experience success.

When you were a student, consider your own learning experiences. Which were successful? What did success do to your attitude toward learning? If you were like most students, you probably were motivated to achieve even more. Peter Davies, the British composer and conductor, said, "Motivation is like food for the brain. You cannot get enough in one sitting. It needs continual and regular top-ups." Success is one factor that gives students these top-ups.

Learning tends to improve as an individual experiences success. Students should be provided successful opportunities, and the sooner the better. Make sure that the first activities you provide are those that will lead to success. Be certain to begin by ensuring short-term success (Elias, 2013).

Classroom application 3.28

Before the school year begins, Ms. Fuller goes out of the way to check her new students' records to determine the content they are ready to learn before she plans curriculum. This information helps her avoid problems immediately by not offering content that is too easy or too difficult so that she can provide the appropriate amount of stress. Not enough stress offers students little or no challenge, and too much stress turns them off (Jensen, 1998).

Ms. Fuller deliberately introduces at the beginning of school some content with which the students are already familiar, and new content in small segments, after which her students experience satisfaction and gain the confidence to continue. She is particularly sensitive to providing initial successful experiences for less able, emotionally challenged, and second-language learners to give them encouragement.

Ms. Fuller is constantly searching for and providing opportunities for all to succeed. She makes a concerted effort to set up an environment in which she teaches for success and communicates a pervasive expectation of progress. She constantly evaluates work and assignments to ensure that students are not involved in busywork but are being challenged at their cognitive levels. When appropriate, Ms. Fuller gives students choices of goals, methods of implementation, and methods of assessment. She uses scoring rubrics as teaching tools to assist students in self-improvement and involves students in constructing the scoring rubrics. For students whose success is slow but progressing, Ms. Fuller tries to improve their success by complimenting them on their *effort*.

NOVELTY

Besides experiencing success, students will continue to be motivated by novelty. The brain likes novelty. It is important not only in the classroom but also in maintaining relationships, job enthusiasm, and purchases (Lyubomirsky, 2012).

Teachers must offer something new periodically to capture and maintain interest. This novelty can come in various ways such as changing seating, the curriculum, locker assignments, room arrangement, or presenting content in new ways. However, just as in providing the appropriate amount of stress when learning new content, there must be a balance between offering novelty and staying with routines.

Classroom application 3.29

Ms. Ross had her students practice their fractions by using worksheets for a few days. She is ready to introduce decimals, so she has her students prepare a ten-inch square, several strips 1x10 inches, and a few 1x1-inch strips. She will have her students use these manipulatives to explore the relationships among 1.0, .1, and .01.

WHAT COMES NEXT?

It is likely that you have watched a TV series that at the end gave a preview of the next episode. If the preview was delivered in an exciting way, it probably raised your curiosity so that you would be motivated to watch the next installment. Students can be motivated when they can anticipate or be curious about what they will learn or do next.

30   Chapter 3

Classroom application 3.30

Ms. Barker: After you learn today how to check blood types, you will check your own blood type and find out which type of blood you can get if you ever need a transfusion. You will also learn the only blood types others may have so that they can safely receive your blood.

Note once again, above, the use of the pronoun *you.*

HIERARCHY OF NEEDS

Motivation psychologist Abraham Maslow (1968, 1970) developed a hierarchy of needs. When examining the hierarchy that follows, you will note that the lowest-level needs are survival needs; the highest-level needs are self-actualization.

>   Self-actualization
>   Esthetic appreciation
>   Intellectual achievement
>   Self-esteem
>   Belonging
>   Safety
>   Survival

According to Maslow:

- humans have wants and desires that influence their behavior;
- unsatisfied needs influence behavior, whereby satisfied needs do not;
- a person's numerous needs are arranged in order of importance, from the basic to the complex;
- a person can progress to the next level of need only after the lower-level need is met;
- the higher a person advances up the hierarchy, the more individuality, humanity, and psychological health will be evident.

In summary, a person is motivated by needs that are unsatisfied. Therefore, he or she will not be motivated to pursue a higher need unless a lower need is met.

Classroom application 3.31

Mr. Lachs has noted that one of his best math students, Terrence, is performing well below expectations. His grades have plummeted, he has not completed homework assignments, and he is not participating in class activities. Mr. Lachs tries to determine what is causing this sudden lack of motivation and performance. His first reaction is deciding what reward he can provide for Terrence. But on further reflection, Mr. Lachs tries to determine any changes in Terrence's life where his lower needs (survival, safety, belonging) are not being fulfilled.

In a personal chat with Terrence, Mr. Lachs discovers that Terrence's mother has lost her job. She has received an eviction notice from the landlord for not paying the rent. His father has not been around in years and is nowhere to be found. Terrence's older sister got a job but was fired for smoking pot. Terrence in only 13 but is looking forward to his next birthday when he can get his working papers and help out.

Mr. Lachs understands that Terrence's anxiety about his family is impeding his interest in school. However, Mr. Lachs is determined that while trying to support Terrence and assuage his feelings and concerns, he will simultaneously not allow Terrence to use his problems as an excuse or reason for not doing as well as his potential will allow.

TEACHER ENTHUSIASM

This chapter on motivation cannot be concluded without reminding you that teachers who show their personal excitement for a lesson also have a better chance of getting their students personally excited and motivated. It is likely that you have been in classrooms where the teacher did not seem to want to be there, or even appeared bored, which made it more difficult for you to feel excited and motivated.

Enthusiasm is contagious, so show enthusiasm. Keep the motivation going by creating a learning environment in which your enthusiasm is picked up by the students.

When students were asked to give their advice to teachers about how to produce an engaging learning environment, one student responded, "Engaging students can be a challenge, and if you're stuck in a monotone, rambling on and on, that doesn't help. . . . Instead of talking like a robot, teachers should speak to us as though they are really passionate about teaching. Make sure to give yourself an attitude check. If a teacher acts like this is the last thing they want to be doing, the kids will respond with the same negative energy. If you act like you want to be there, then we will too" (Wolpert-Gawron, 2012).

SELF-REFLECTION

- Which of your students are intrinsically motivated?
- How long did it take for you to learn your students' names?
- How long did it take for you to call them by name?

- How long did it take for students to address each other by name?
- What do you know about what your students already know?
- What did you do recently to ensure that your students were ready for instruction?
- How much do you know about your students' interests?
- How have you used that knowledge in the classroom?
- What have you done that shows you are enthusiastic about teaching?
- How do you ensure that your students are successful?
- Think about some lessons you have taught recently. What could you have done to improve them using the examples in this chapter?
- What are you planning to teach in the near future? How will you integrate the ideas illustrated in this chapter into your teaching?

Chapter Four

Setting Goals/Objectives and Obtaining Feedback

How many times have you been in a classroom when you asked yourself, "What is the point?", "What is this leading to?", or "What am I doing here?" How did you react to not knowing where the lesson (class) was going?

GOALS AND OBJECTIVES

There is an overwhelming amount of research that shows that students who are aware of goals and objectives of instruction are highly likely to achieve them. When there is a purpose in learning something, especially when the goal is *personally* important to learners, they will probably become ego involved and thus succeed. Objectives should be made clear to the students in *every* lesson unless the objective itself is to discover the objective. Goals and objectives are important because they will help both you and your students determine how successful your teaching and their learning have been.

When determining goals and objectives, students must be ready, willing, and able to receive the instruction (Ryan, Cooper, & Tauer, 2008). Students must be prepared with prerequisite knowledge and/or experience that will serve as a foundation for the new information. Since they are constantly being bombarded with competing stimuli, students will select those that are interesting and stay with those that are enjoyable.

There is a difference between goals and objectives. In general, goals are outcomes (results) of instruction expressed as long-term statements regarding what the students will accomplish. Standards are examples of goals. Goals state what the students should accomplish with respect to the content by the end of a unit, semester, or year. Obviously, goals are not accomplished in a day. They clearly offer direction and overall thrust to instruction within its time frame.

Though you may have your own goals in planning and teaching a unit, goals should not emphasize what you want to achieve, but what you want the *students* to achieve. When age appropriate, *students should also determine, in addition to your goals, their own goals* to accomplish by the end of the unit.

It is valuable to write a rubric for each goal. Dr. Robert Marzano has developed a free scale bank, a most valuable tool that both teachers and students can use for assessing the achievement of any Common Core State Standard at various points in the instructional process. To view the scale bank, go to http://www.marzanoresearch.com. Click on Free Resources, then on Proficiency Scale Bank. Register and then complete the information regarding the standard on which you are working and the corresponding assessment scale, as indicated by scores, will be produced.

Objectives are frequently referred to interchangeably in curriculum literature as behavioral objectives, instructional, or performance objectives. (Those that are referred to as educational objectives are often actually goals because, even though they include the word objective, educational objectives are achievable over a longer period of time.)

Objectives derive their content from goals and, as opposed to goals, are achievable in the short term, usually within a lesson. Objectives are written to communicate clearly to students what they are expected to achieve. This communication is particularly important, because as already indicated, and verified by brain research (Jensen, 1998), students who are aware of goals and objectives are more likely to attain them.

FEEDBACK

Goals and objectives cannot be discussed adequately unless the discussion includes feedback regarding those goals and objectives. Feedback means knowledge of results, and the sooner the student receives feedback the better.

When were you particularly interested in knowing how well you performed on a test? Probably immediately after taking the test. Several days or a week later you were likely to have lost interest.

Goals/objectives and feedback complement each other. The late former mayor of New York City, Ed Koch, used to travel frequently around the city's five boroughs asking residents, "How am I doing?" Obviously, he needed this feedback from them so that he could change what he was doing and make improvements *before* it was too late.

Students need to be constantly informed of their progress (obtain feedback), especially in knowing where their errors are. Quick knowledge of results allows students to correct errors before they become consistent. This knowledge is of particular importance in an era in which self-efficacy is being promoted as a positive goal. Students should feel that they have control over their learning so that they are able to deal effectively with a task to which they have been assigned.

You should note that students would rather know their answer was incorrect (receive negative feedback) than have no knowledge of results at all (receive no feedback).

Feedback is necessary so that all along the way teachers can assess and students self-assess by tracking their progress on achievement. This feedback must be ascertained to decide what, if necessary, could have been done differently to achieve goals and objectives and what can be done differently in the future. This is growth at its best.

Research is clear that the frequency of assessments increases achievement (Marzano, 2007). Assessments can be informal or formal. Informal assessments include observing performance on homework and classroom assignments; student participation in classroom discussions; samples of student work; student feedback; student-to-student and student-to-teacher interaction; or performance on quizzes. Formal assessments usually include the use of standardized tests, pre-tests, classroom tests, portfolios, and performance tasks, projects, and presentations.

Students should keep a log to monitor their progress. Periodically, teachers should discuss this log with the student, in particular to determine whether there needs to be an adjustment in input on the part of the teacher, the student, or both.

Above all, it is important to celebrate student achievement, even if it is a very small gain (Marzano, 2007).

Classroom application 4.1

Ms. Donaldson is a Family and Consumer Science teacher. She has a group of twenty-two 10th and 11th graders in her class. She has prepared a unit for them, Improving Wellness with the Dietary Guidelines. In preparing the unit goals, Ms. Donaldson has tried to phrase them in a personal way. She knows that when learning is personalized, students are more motivated (Chapter 3). Her unit goals are:

- Apply *your* knowledge of food choices and menus to plan a balanced diet
- Use new technologies to plan and prepare nutritious meals for a variety of dietary needs
- Adjust *your* own diet to accommodate changing levels of activity or to meet *your* nutritional needs throughout the life cycle
- Identify ways to meet basic needs of all *your* family members

- Take reasoned action toward reaching *personal* health goals

Ms. Donaldson explains the goals to the class. She already has a poster in the front of the room displaying the goals. On another poster she presents the same goals as questions.

After explaining the goals, Ms. Donaldson asks the class to write in their diaries their own personal goals regarding this unit. She communicates to the class that if they do not have any identified personal goals now, they can add them as the unit progresses.

Some of the personal goals her students came up with are:

- Analyze how my culture's dietary habits (African American, in this case) affect health and longevity
- Adjust my recipes to keep them tasty while maintaining good nutrition
- Help my friends get off junk food and eat healthier

As soon as Ms. Donaldson believes that the goals are clear, she introduces some ideas regarding how the students will be evaluated. These evaluations include:

- written analysis of *your* own diet utilizing the 2010 Dietary Guidelines for Americans,
- designing a five-day diet for another student of *your* choice in the class, taking into account the person's individual dietary/health needs; age; caloric level; weight; activity level; food likes and dislikes; and dietary habits.
- preparing a self-evaluation of the unit: What did *you* learn from this unit? How will *you* alter *your* own dietary habits as a result of this learning experience? What topics from this unit would *you* like to learn more about?
- an oral presentation on a selected topic. The rubric for this oral presentation is eventually designed by *both* the students and Ms. Donaldson. She involves the students because she wants them to internalize the criteria and have them clear and present in their minds before they begin preparing that oral presentation.

Wiggins and McTighe (1998, 2005), two leaders in the field of assessment, suggest that samples of students' and professionals' work should be analyzed first to determine what range of excellence they demonstrate. It is essential that rubrics be constructed on the basis of the absolute best possible performance, because if they are constructed the way students are currently performing, the students will remain at that performance level.

Once the best performance is determined, then minimal performance should be identified. After both the poorest and best performances are described, intermediate levels between the two are determined, and a scoring rubric can then be presented quantitatively as a scale. The scale can range from 1 to 4 or 1 to 10 with the most common scoring rubric presenting a scale from 1 to 6, with 1 as the lowest level of performance and 6 the highest.

Scoring rubrics may also be expressed qualitatively as poor through outstanding, novice through professional, emergent through fluent, or any other equivalent system depending on the type of performance being assessed. It is recommended that the number of categories in the quantitative or qualitative scale be **even** because judgment tends toward the center. If a scale of 1 to 5 is used, many evaluators, even with specific criteria, will tend to select the midpoint, 3.

Corresponding to each point or level on a scale is a set of performance descriptors which indicates clearly what criteria must be demonstrated to qualify for that score. Criteria should always be described in positive terms what the performance was, avoiding what the performance was not. For example, a descriptor such as "made basic computational errors" would be better than stating, "did not have the ability to compute basic problems."

The criteria should not be evaluative (fair, good, excellent) and should discriminate sufficiently from each other so that each level of achievement can be distinguished with no overlapping. Clear, discriminating criteria give validity to the rubric; specificity and observability give reliability to the rubric.

Classroom application 4.1 (continued)

Ms. Donaldson used this rubric, prepared with her students, for her improving wellness unit.

Oral Presentation Rubric

Score of 4

- Clearly indicates preparation in an organized manner with a beginning (introduction), a body of knowledge, and logical conclusions and summary
- Presents in a clear voice and can be heard by all in the class
- Demonstrates enthusiasm and personal interest in the topic
- Shows little reliance on notes
- Actively engages all members of the group
- Utilizes proper cooking terminology and explanation of vocabulary
- Uses visual aids to highlight key points
- Fields questions competently

Score of 3

- Clearly indicates preparation in an organized manner with a beginning (introduction), a body of knowledge, and logical conclusions and summary

- Presents in a clear voice and can be heard by all in the class
- Demonstrates enthusiasm and personal interest in the topic
- Is too dependent on notes
- Engages just a few members of the group
- Utilizes proper cooking terminology and explanation of vocabulary
- Uses visual aids to highlight key points
- Fields questions with some uncertainty

Score of 2

- Presentation shows signs of disorganization
- Speaker is difficult to hear, speaks at an inappropriate pace, and shows little enthusiasm
- Uses proper cooking terminology but avoids explanation of vocabulary
- Is too dependent on notes
- Involves only a few students and fields questions with hesitation

Score of 1

- Lacks understanding of central project theme as evidenced by a disorganized presentation
- Speaker seems insecure about asking and answering questions
- Speaker is difficult to hear and lacks enthusiasm
- Is too dependent on notes

As the unit progresses, Ms. Donaldson has the students periodically monitor their progress (feedback) toward achieving the goals. If necessary, she adjusts her instruction, and/or her students *modify their own learning tactics* for the purpose of achieving the goal.

Ms. Donaldson gathers information for any adjustments that may be necessary by classroom observations; informal questions; discussions; quizzes; and performance on assignments. (Adapted from the unit "Improving Wellness with the Dietary Guidelines," prepared by Patricia Donaldson with permission of the author.)

Once unit goals are decided, they are broken down into objectives. One or more related objectives are then taught in specific lessons.

PRIMING THE BRAIN REVISITED

According to brain research, there is no learning without memory and that memory depends on attention (Jensen, 1998). So how do you get that attention? During the anticipatory set (Chapter 3) you make students aware of and hooked into the objective. It is your opportunity to stimulate the students' curiosity.

Brain research tells us that the brain can be primed, and if the students know (are primed with) the objective, chances are that they will achieve it. And since the brain is always paying attention to something, the anticipatory set is your opportunity to concentrate the students' attention on the lesson by thwarting competing stimuli.

The anticipatory set provides *motivation* for gaining this attention. Motivation, you will recall from Chapter 3, introduces enough frustration to make the students want to go back into equilibrium, and the "going back into equilibrium" is the activity in which learning takes place. ". . . significant learning is frequently accompanied or impelled by discomfort" (Joyce, Weil, & Calhoun, 2004).

Students should be informed regarding why the objective is important and what it means to them *personally*. Assuming that the students can read, many teachers find that once the objective is elicited, an effective practice is writing it on the board or on a poster.

Displaying the objective helps keep the students focused on where they are heading and provides a link to eventually closing the lesson. In addition, as already mentioned, knowing the objective assists students in self-assessing.

Some teachers find it helpful to write the objective in the form of a question. "To calculate the area of a circle" would then become, "How can you calculate the area of a circle?" (Notice how the question uses the pronoun *you*.) At the end of the lesson the students would then decide whether or not they could answer the question adequately.

It is also important for you to know whether or not the students are aware of the objective. Just because you state it or one or more of the students can state the objective does not mean that everyone is aware of it. You will have a better handle on knowing how aware the students are of the objective if you have several students repeat the objective not in parrot form but *in their own words*.

Revisit the end of the first classroom application, 3.1, presented by Mr. Jacobs in the previous chapter.

Mr. Jacobs: Good guesses, but in my lunch box is *another* lunch box.

[The students all look at each other with puzzled faces (discomfort level), obviously having been thrown off balance. Mr. Jacobs opens his lunch box. The students look with anticipation. In the lunch box is a lima bean. He places the lima bean on his desk.] So what do you think we are going to learn today? [There is a long pause as Mr. Jacobs observes the still crinkled faces.] Debbie.

Debbie: How . . . how or why a lima bean is a lunch box?

Mr. Jacobs: Excellent, Debbie, now who can say that in another way? Jerry.

Jerry: How a lunch box and a lima bean are the same.

Mr. Jacobs: Great, Jerry. Give us a different way of saying this. Paul.

Paul: How is a lima bean like lunch?

At this point Mr. Jacobs writes the objective on the board in two ways. First he writes "to discover how a lima bean is like a lunch box" and then he writes, taking Paul's question, "How is a lima bean like lunch?"

SEQUENCING OBJECTIVES

Once an objective for a lesson is decided, it may be necessary to break that objective down into component objectives. This process is particularly critical when *sequence* is important. Breaking down the objective also provides an assessment (feedback) for both you and students in determining how well they are progressing in achieving the main objective.

Classroom application 4.2

Mr. Roberts is teaching a lesson on the digestive system. His main objective for the lesson is: the student will be able to describe the digestive process. This is what his students will do at the *end* of the lesson. He then arranges this objective into a sequence of smaller objectives that will lead the students to describing the digestive process. He arranges the content so that it makes sense to the learner. For his students to be able to describe the digestive process, they have to be able to:

1. explain the function of digestion
2. identify the organs in the digestive system
3. locate the organs in the digestive system
4. describe the function of each organ
5. trace different food particles through the digestive system

Mr. Roberts turns the objectives into corresponding questions.

1. What is the main purpose of the digestive system?
2. Which organs are in the digestive system?
3. Where are these organs located?
4. What is the job of each organ?

5. How does a food particle travel through the digestive system and what happens to it along the way?

Mr. Roberts knows that these five objectives sequentially and collectively describe the digestive process—his lesson objective. Those of his students who cannot identify the organs will not be able to describe their function. Any student who cannot locate the organs will not be able to trace food through them.

Mr. Roberts has obtained a life-size model of the human body for his students. This model not only displays the organs in each system but also allows the students to observe the location of digestive system organs relative to each other and to other organs in the body.

Writing smaller intermittent objectives from a main objective is often a difficult process for teachers, one that takes practice. But the identification of these objectives tells you where to begin after the anticipatory set. These sequential objectives also assist in helping you design an assessment (feedback) for the attainment of these objectives as the students proceed and, therefore, whether or not you or they need to adjust instruction along the way. The *paired* objective and assessment provide a guide to what instructional input would be most appropriate in achieving the objective (Chapter 5). Also, having a clear idea of the sequence of instruction, when sequence is necessary, avoids the problem of sometimes "losing" the students when a *critical* step in the learning process is omitted.

To summarize, objectives are the *results* of instruction. Once you have decided the main objective, the intermittent objectives that will lead to it, and how each will be assessed, you will be in a better position to decide the most effective learning experiences the students should have in order to meet each assessment.

At this point it would be valuable to reemphasize that merely exposing students to different activities, no matter how exciting and dynamic they are, will not produce their desired results unless *the students know the purpose* of those activities (Nuthall & Alton-Lee, 1993; Nuthall, 1999).

In this age of standards, and with the Common Core State Standards designed to prepare students for college and careers (Pagliaro, 2012), it is worthwhile to emphasize **college** as a goal, *especially for those who might not ever have considered it*. Having college as a goal that is promoted and encouraged by teachers could go a long way to having students reassess their direction in life.

ERROR ANALYSIS

Feedback can also be obtained through error analysis. Error analysis is the study of mistakes made by students and the frequency of their occurrence. Errors should be of concern when they are persistent, showing a real lack of understanding and not just carelessness.

Error analysis is useful to both the teacher and the student. If enough students make the same error, this feedback should serve as a signal for the teacher to change instruction to make the original instruction more effective. When a student makes an error repeatedly, the student should be made aware of the error so that he or she can remediate it.

Whenever possible, students should learn to identify their own errors and self-correct them so that errors do not become habitual. Students can be given correct answers, especially for mathematics problems, to check their work and see if they can come up with their own error diagnosis and corrections.

Currently, it is a common practice to have students correct each other's work, and when the situation permits, have a student explain to the student making an error why it is incorrect. It would then be incumbent on the student who made the error to create an example of a new situation where the error is not repeated.

Steiny (2010) has described the way she has students learn from their errors. She distributes a standard form with three squares across a large grid. In the first box the students rewrite the problem (or question that had the error). In the second box they determine what they did wrong by describing the misunderstanding. And finally, in the third box, they redo the problem (correct the error).

On the basis of the analysis, all or some of the students can move on, or the content can be retaught in a different way for those in need. One of the pervasive criticisms of remedial instruction is that during remediation, students are exposed to the *same methodology* that was ineffective for them in the first place.

Cotton (2000) has researched validated approaches to reteaching. One of these approaches is, "Using different materials and strategies for re-teaching than those used for initial instruction, rather than merely providing a 'rehash' of previously taught lessons" (p. 26).

Brookhart (2012) emphasizes the importance of the clarity of the target (goal) in learning the content or a skill. She states that when there is a mismatch between the learning target and performance of understanding, ". . . students often experience feedback as evaluation or grading rather than information for improvement" (p. 26). She identifies effective feedback as timely, while there is still time to change; descriptive of the work to be accomplished, as opposed to the student personally; positive, building on strengths and showing how to improve weakness; clear and specific so the student knows how to move on; and differentiated so that each student knows what to do regarding the current assignment, which may range from simple reminders to prompts, examples, or complete revisions.

Classroom application 4.3

Ms. Sharp has noticed that Beth has handed in a paper with the following errors:

```
350           408           381
x12           x23           x44
700          1224          1524
350           816          1524
1050         3058          3084
```

Ms. Sharp understands that it is not enough to tell Beth that she has made mistakes, or that she needs help in math. The feedback must be *specific* or it is useless. Obviously, Beth needs instruction and practice in place value.

First, Ms. Sharp obtains feedback from Beth regarding what she thinks her understanding or lack of understanding is. Then not only will Ms. Sharp deliver this instruction in a *different* way from the one to which Beth was exposed the first time, but she will give Beth a *strategy* to deal with the error. Beth will write the initial problems and separate the ones, tens, and hundreds with vertical line segments which she will label. She will determine whether her responses correspond with the labeled headings. Then Ms. Sharp will have Benny, a student who has mastered place value, help Beth should she need continued support.

Ms. Sharp also notes that Beth, and perhaps other students, need help in approximating answers to see if their answers are reasonable. For instance, in the first example, 350 x 12, if 2 x 350 is 700, is it possible for 12 x 350 to be only 1050, Beth's answer to the first problem?

Another type of error students frequently make involves grammar.

Classroom application 4.4

Mr. Buono noted that most of his students had the same type of error as that in the following:
    Each boy had their time to pick a topic.
Mr. Buono knew that his students needed instruction in agreement between nouns and their representative pronouns. Singular nouns need corresponding singular pronouns. After this instruction he handed his students a story with a mixture of correct and incorrect pronouns regarding their noun antecedents. Then he had

his students correct the pronouns that did not agree with their antecedent nouns. When he was confident that the students had mastered the content, he had them write their own compositions with a mixture of correct and incorrect pronouns to challenge their classmates to identify the mistakes.

Students in special education classes may tend to have more errors.

Classroom application 4.5

Ms. O'Connor teaches a special education class. She received this writing sample from one of her students—a 10-year-old fourth-grade boy. The writing was performed after reading a story in which Native Americans attacked Pilgrims in their homes and set these homes on fire. The Pilgrims retaliated by shooting at the Native Americans.

> I think the book was grate my favorite part was when he fired the gun I also like the Illustrashuns. They look so real. My favorite picture is when he fired the gun. That is why when he fired the gun is my favorite part. Because of the illastrashons.

Ms. O'Connor examined the writing by answering the following questions she began to implement after reading Wiggins (1996). She asked several other fourth-grade teachers to read the sample writing and give their input.

- "What knowledge seems to be firmly acquired?"
- "Where are there persistent errors/misconceptions?"
- "What prerequisite knowledge had not been mastered that allowed errors/misconceptions to occur?"
- "How can these errors/misconceptions be remediated?"

Ms. O'Connor and her colleagues determined that her student needs remediation in sentence structure; homophones; spelling; capitalization; grammar; and idea expansion. This remediation is no small challenge.

Examining samples of student work in *all* subjects is a productive way to perform diagnostic teaching by analyzing errors and determining understanding as well as misunderstanding. This examination is most effective when it is performed collaboratively with other teachers.

In summary, Csikszentmihalyi (1990), the Hungarian psychologist, has emphasized the importance of flow, intrinsic motivation that produces the desire to engage in a challenging task. He has offered three conditions that produce this state of flow.

1. Presenting clear goals

2. Offering goals that are achievable and within one's ability and skill set, with both being at a high level.
3. Providing clear and instant feedback so that, if necessary, the course for attaining the goals can be adjusted.

TEACHER ASSESSMENT

This chapter cannot be concluded unless teacher assessment is mentioned. Teacher assessment includes not only feedback to teachers by students but teacher self-assessment. Teachers frequently get feedback on their performance by having students evaluate them in writing regarding what could have been done differently to make instruction more productive. Some teachers video record themselves and play the video for the students. Then the students discuss not only what could have been done to improve teacher performance but also what could have been done to improve their performance.

SELF-REFLECTION

- What are the differences between goals and objectives?
- How do you make your students aware of goals?
- How do you make your students aware of objectives?
- When did you have your students determine their own goals?
- How do you provide feedback to your students?
- How often do you provide feedback to your students?
- How do you use rubrics in your classroom?
- If age-appropriate, are your students involved in constructing rubrics?
- Examine the rubrics you have used. How do they meet the criteria for rubric construction presented in this chapter?
- How do you use feedback to make students responsible for their own learning?
- How frequently do you analyze samples of student work?
- When have you involved your colleagues in analyzing these samples?
- What persistent student errors have you noted?
- How did you remediate those errors by reteaching the content in a **different** way?
- What will you do differently in the future as a result of reading this chapter?

Chapter Five

Engaging Students in New Learning

It must be restated that goals and objectives should be decided after the teacher is confident of the prior knowledge/readiness of the students, the background information/experiences they possess as a scaffold onto which they can proceed with and hook into new learning. Only then can learning experiences (input) to deliver that new knowledge be selected.

Once you have decided the main objective, the intermittent objectives that will lead to it, and how each will be assessed, you will be in a better position to decide the most effective learning experiences the students should have in order to meet each assessment. To help you decide, ask the questions that follow.

QUESTIONS TO ASK IN SELECTING INSTRUCTIONAL ACTIVITIES

Q1. Does the objective involve semantic knowledge, that which is concerned with meaning?

If so, is the meaning

- a concept—a category that groups similar things such as a noun, vertebrate, or government;
- a principle—a generalization that states relationships between two or among several concepts, such as a rule or a law like "i before e except after c"; or
- an attitude, such as respect for the culture of others?

Q2. Does the objective involve procedural knowledge, that which is intended to develop the performance of a task or skill?

If so, is the skill

- cognitive (a mathematical computation);
- social (exhibiting positive behavior to others who are different);
- or physical (setting up and using a microscope)?

Q3. Does the objective involve a combination of the above?

You will note in Table 5.1 that several strategies such as problem solving and discovery are listed in several columns and can cover different learning outcomes. Your challenge here is keeping the students' attention, and keeping them meaningfully engaged. (A comprehensive review of engaged learning has been conducted by the North Central Regional Educational Laboratory. You can access this information at http://www.ncrel.org/sdrs/engaged.htm.)

To reiterate, regarding the instructional strategy, ". . . the most effective instruction is that which addresses multiple modalities: instruction where

Table 5.1. INSTRUCTIONAL STRATEGIES AND THEIR LEARNING OUTCOMES

CONCEPTS/PRINCIPLES	SKILLS	ATTITUDES/SOCIAL DEVELOPMENT
Lectures	Drill and practice	Role playing
Debates	Computer-assisted instruction	Dramas
Panels	Modeling	Cooperative learning
Videos	Demonstrations	Discussions
Guest speakers	Games/simulations	Videos
Discovery	Independent study	Problem solving
Internet research		Games/simulations
Concept attainment		Debates
Concept formation		Case studies
Advance organizers		Discovery
Mastery learning/contracts		
Cooperative learning		
Learning activity centers		
Case studies		
Problem solving		
Demonstrations		
Dramas		
Discussions		
Games/simulations		
Independent study		

students get to hear, see, touch, and discuss. . . . There is no one best way" (Hunter, 2004, p. 7).

Sometimes each intermittent objective, assessment, and learning experience (input, strategy) needs a one-to-one correspondence. In other cases the same assessment and learning experience can cover several objectives.

The way new material is first encoded is critical. When new material is "processed" in a confused or incorrect manner, the student does not have the option of pressing a delete button, but must "unprocess" the material.

There are many ways to assist students with learning original material more effectively.

KWLH

Some teachers use the KWLH method when introducing new content. Students indicate in writing what they already **K**now about a topic. Then they state what they **W**ould like to learn about the topic. The first two parts of this strategy give students the opportunity to preview new content before they proceed with actual implementation. This information can be part of your diagnostic evaluation because the information is valuable in assisting you in deciding if parts of the content you originally planned to cover should be modified. Students can also ask questions about the content before you begin instruction. When students complete the study of the content, they indicate what they have actually **L**earned. And finally, students then identify **H**ow they can learn more.

VIVID EXPERIENCES

Learning is understood better and remembered longer if the original experience with the content is *vivid*. Vivid experiences gain attention and have a greater *impact* on the learner. They include the use of color, surprise, loudness, music, or physical activity to convey a message. The advertising industry is well versed in using these experiences in getting their products or services across. Observe the use of these experiences the next time you view a commercial on TV.

Classroom application 5.1

After her class has spent a considerable time working with manipulatives, Ms. Clark places a bright-colored and decorated number line on her classroom floor. She writes the following equation on the whiteboard
$$2 + 3 = ?$$

and asks for volunteers, finally calling on Jamie to "jump" the equation on the number line beginning at 0 while simultaneously stating the jumps. Jamie says, "Two jumps plus three jumps equals five jumps." Ms. Clark then erases the "?" and completes the equation on the board. She adds more equations and calls on several other students whose jumps are verbalized and also recorded. Then Ms. Clark erases the sums and calls on students to complete them without the number line. Ms. Clark knows that students can learn and remember addition facts more effectively using this physical activity than by completing worksheets.

Classroom application 5.2

Mr. Sullivan is teaching contractions.

> Mr. Sullivan: What does the word "contract" mean? [He gestures the word as he says it.] Janelle.
>
> Janelle: Make smaller.
>
> Mr. Sullivan: Good. [He gestures contract again.] Now who can say it another way?
>
> Randy: Shrink.
>
> Mr. Sullivan: Yes, contract means make smaller, shorten, or shrink. And today we are going to make words smaller.

[He has prepared large cards, each displaying one letter of the alphabet for words he intends to use, duplicate cards for each letter, and a card with an apostrophe. He gives each of five students one card. Each card has one of the five letters in the words, do not. Mr. Sullivan lines up the students so that they face the class while holding up their letters in the order, d o n o t, making sure that there is a larger space between the two words than there is between the letters. He gives an additional student, Fred, an apostrophe card and instructs Fred to physically (but gently) push away any letters and stand in their place to form a short version of the words. He pushes the o in "not" away and stands where the o originally was. Using an exaggerated physical movement, Mr. Sullivan then pushes all the remaining letters closer to each other.]

> Mr. Sullivan: Fred, what did you just do?
>
> Fred: I pushed o away and now I'm where it was.
>
> Mr. Sullivan: Which o did you push away?
>
> Fred: The o in not.

Mr. Sullivan: What contraction did you make?

Fred: I replaced a letter with an apostrophe.

Mr. Sullivan: What specific contraction did you make?

Fred: I made don't out of do not.

Mr. Sullivan: What do you think may be the general contraction rule?

Fred: When you shorten two words, put an apostrophe where the letters are taken away.

Mr. Sullivan: Who else can state the rule?

[He calls on several students. Then he offers more examples where students are each given a letter of the original words, one an apostrophe, and asked to make the contractions. Finally, he asks the class to come up with their own examples.]

It should be obvious that learning about contractions was made more *vivid* by the physical activity and visuals associated with it.

Recent housing foreclosures, short sales, and accumulating credit card debt have made it obvious that the public in general is not well versed in finance. It is not unusual for people to think that if they do not have children in school, their real estate taxes do not go to education, or if they have a 30-year mortgage, they have already paid off half their house in 15 years. Many people do not know what their insurance policies cover, or equally important, what they do not cover. Then when an unfortunate unanticipated incident occurs, these people find themselves paying a lot of money for uncovered liabilities.

There are some who believe that inadequate education fosters debt and leads to a misunderstanding of money matters in general (Dvorkin, 2012). This lack of knowledge may carry over to our nation's difficulty in handling its own debt. Moreover, there seems to be a casual indifference to acquiring this knowledge.

This situation has become so critical that the United States Treasury Department has developed a website, www.MoneyAsYouLearn.org, to provide teachers with prepared personal finance lessons. These lessons were designed to complement math and English courses and are aligned with the Common Core State Standards (Duffy, 2013; Kadlec, 2013).

Mr. Fein finds that poor understanding of money matters in general is also prevalent in the affluent community in which he teaches. Though he is an English teacher, not a math or economics teacher, Mr. Fein decides he is going to do something about this lack of financial awareness the moment an occasion arises, and he wants the experience to be vivid by *making the abstract concrete*.

Classroom application 5.3

Mr. Fein overhears one of his students, Karen, telling classmates that her family just renovated their kitchen and bathrooms at a cost of $125,000. Karen and her friends seem to speak nonchalantly about this amount of money. Mr. Fein also knows that Karen has bragged about her job as a lifeguard over the summer and spending her salary on clothes. A few days later Karen tells him about the renovation and its cost.

Mr. Fein: Do you realize how much money this is, Karen?

(She looks at him in such a way that he is not sure if she is saying, "Mind your own business" or "I don't care or have a clue.")

Mr. Fein: You mentioned that this summer you had a job as a lifeguard.

Karen: Yeah.

Mr. Fein: What was your salary?

Karen: Ten dollars an hour.

Mr. Fein: Wow, that's higher than minimum wage. How many hours did you work?

Karen: Forty hours a week, that was the most they allowed.

Mr. Fein: How many weeks?

Karen: [Thinks for a while.] Nine.

Mr. Fein: So how many hours was that in total?

Karen: Let's see. Forty times nine. Three hundred sixty.

Mr. Fein: At $10 per hour, how much did you make for the summer?

Karen: $3,600.

Mr. Fein: Did you save any of the money, maybe for college?

Karen: Save? No, I bought clothes.

Engaging Students in New Learning

Mr. Fein: [Scratches his head.] Making that same amount each summer, how many summers would you have to work to get $125,000?

Karen: [Tries to estimate, then takes her calculator from her backpack.] More than 34. [She says this looking completely surprised.]

Mr. Fein: Suppose that was your full-time job and you worked 50 weeks a year as most people do, how much would you earn in one year?

Karen: [She fiddles with her calculator once again.] $20,800.

Mr. Fein: With that amount, how long would it take you to earn $125,000?

Karen: More than six years. [This time she says this without the assistance of the calculator.]

Mr. Fein: You bet, and $20,800 is the money you would have, not only for clothes but for food, shelter, or anything else you needed. And people who make much more than that have to pay taxes, so what was left would have to pay for their expenses.

Karen: What? Never thought about it that way.

Mr. Fein: Well, take *extra* good care of the kitchen and bathrooms.

Mr. Walter was frustrated with the public's general lack of understanding of the nation's $17 trillion debt and counting. His frustration reached its peak when he heard one of his 12th-grade American government students speaking about the debt say, "What are a few more zeroes?" How could he make their understanding of the debt *vivid*?

Classroom application 5.4

Mr. Walter: How many think you know what a trillion is? [Many hands go up.] Jill.

Jill: A one with twelve zeroes.

Mr. Walter: [Writes 1,000,000,000,000 on the whiteboard.] Who can say it another way?

Luke: A billion with three zeroes after it.

Mr. Walter: That's also correct, how else can we say this?

Lourdes: A thousand billion. Uh, Uh, and a hundred thousand million.

Mr. Walter: [Records these also. He elicits a few more interpretations and continues to record those that are correct on the whiteboard.] Let me ask you this in yet a different way. Suppose I asked you to go back in time. How long ago would a trillion seconds be? Think about it for a while and take a guess. [He records some of their responses. They range from three weeks to 50 years ago.]

Mr. Walter: See if you can actually compute this. I will give you time to make the calculation. [He waits several minutes as the students try to make the computation.]

Sam: I did this twice and got the same answer but it can't be right.

Mr. Walter: What did you get?

Sam: 31,709 years ago, 32,000, rounded off to the nearest thousand, can that be?

Mr. Walter: That's right, Sam. Neanderthals were roaming the plains of Europe 32,000 years ago. A trillion seconds ago is way before any of the civilizations you have studied existed. And consider our nation. It is less than 300 years old. Now think about it this way. [Mr. Walter is armed with other data which he states and lists on the whiteboard.]

Mr. Walter: If I made $480 million per hour working 40 hours a week, I would have $1 trillion after one year. If everybody on the planet got on a giant scale, the scale would record 1 trillion pounds. One trillion days ago would be the year 2,739,725,168 BC (assuming the date beginning the calculation is September 5, 2012). If I had 1 trillion bricks, I could build the Great Wall of China 258 times. [Mr. Walter is quick to add.] So far we are talking about 1 trillion. Imagine what it would be if, like our national debt, it would be more than 17 trillion. And that does not include interest on the debt. We also have 86 trillion, and I repeat trillion with a t, of unfunded liabilities. And guess who is going to have to pay for all of this?

[Mr. Walter is satisfied that the abstract has been made concrete and the class is armed for a discussion.] (Santelli, 2012).

PREVIEWING CONTENT

Original content is processed more efficiently if it is *previewed* before actual instruction begins.

Classroom application 5.5

Mr. Griffin teaches general science. Before he begins he wants to give his students an overview as well as a preview of the sciences and how they are distinct from one another. Mr. Griffin presents his students with an advance organizer (Figure 5.1).

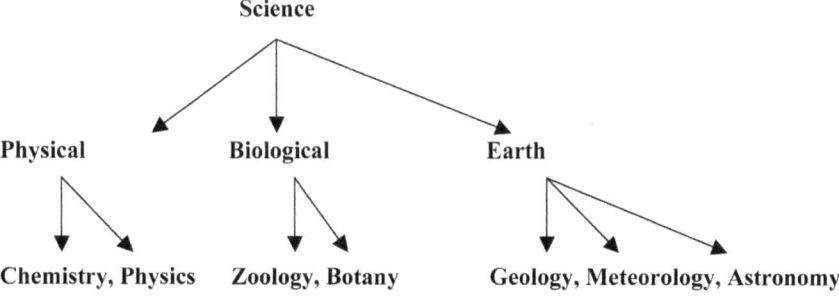

Figure 5.1.

First he asks the students if they can identify differences. Generally they indicate that chemistry is concerned with what substances are made of. Most of the students know that biology is the study of living things. Since many of the students have visited a zoo, they know that zoology is the study of animals. Some students infer that since the other living thing besides animals is plants, botany must be the study of plants. Almost all the students know what geology, meteorology, and astronomy are. But Mr. Griffin helps the students distinguish among these three by stating that geology studies what is going on under the earth, meteorology studies what is happening just above the earth in the earth's atmosphere, and astronomy, way above the earth outside the earth's atmosphere.

CONTRAST

Original learning can be improved with *contrast*. The more strongly one part of a situation contrasts with another, the more likely a student is to remember it. Students understand and remember situations that are different, those that are exceptions or stand out.

Classroom application 5.6

Ms. Sanders is teaching spelling. She emphasizes that the only word in the English language that ends in "sede" is supersede. Knowing this makes it easier for her students *not* to spell –cede words, such as accede or secede, with a "sede" ending or supersede itself as supercede, which is commonly done.

Another difference is that, of the words that the class is studying, all right, usually misspelled as alright, is the only one that is *always* two words.

When teaching the spelling rule that in forming the past tense in some verbs that end in a consonant, double the consonant and add *ed*, Ms. Sanders knows that her students will remember the rule better if the letters involved in the change are enlarged and colored.

Present Tense	Past Tense
stop	stoPPed

Classroom application 5.7

Ms. Minton teaches foreign languages, French and Italian. Whenever the occasion arises, she is careful to point out *differences* (contrast) between those languages and English, and between those languages themselves.

Ms. Minton: When using the negative, it is acceptable in those languages to use the double negative. However, in English it is incorrect to use the double negative. I didn't do nothing is incorrect. Listen to how more logical the English version is, because if you did not do nothing, then you did something. [She gives her students time to think about and absorb the logic. Ms. Minton always points out other differences.]

Ms. Minton: In Italian, the word cheese is *for*maggio but in French it is *fro*mage.

She asks the students to make up a memory device that has meaning to them so that they can remember the difference. One student wrote, "I am *for* Italian cheese but run away *from* French cheese."

MEMORY

Willingham (2009) suggests that when teaching new content you should remember the memory model you likely studied in an introductory psychology and/or an educational psychology course.

Sensory Memory→→→Working Memory→→→Long-Term Memory

(Incoming   (Location of awareness   (Location of factual and
environmental stimuli)   and thinking)   procedural knowledge)

Environmental stimuli contain effects you can hear and see as well as problems to be solved. These sensory stimuli are the initial processing that converts these incoming stimuli into information from which we can make sense. Though our capacity for storing sensory stimuli in sensory memory is large, it doesn't hold these stimuli very long, most frequently between one and three seconds.

Working memory contains the content you are *currently* thinking about or are aware of. This content could include seeing lightning, hearing the sound of thunder, a motorcycle, or a neighbor's lawn mower.

Long-term memory is the huge warehouse where you keep the factual knowledge you have acquired: a caterpillar turns into a butterfly, George Washington was the first president of the United States, the hypotenuse of a right triangle can be found by calculating the square root of the sum of the squares of its other two sides. You are not aware of this long-term information which remains dormant until called upon to enter working memory. Then this information enters your consciousness.

Since students can consider only a limited amount of information at one time, teachers should not overload the students' working memories. When asking students to consider problems/instruction that involve multiple steps, whether these problems are mathematical, logical, or involve new concept application, teachers should try to judge the appropriate pace for presenting this information. Memory devices such as prepared posters or the chalkboard/smartboard/whiteboard should be incorporated so that the information can be recalled from these instead of having to keep it in the students' current awareness (Baddeley, 2007).

Classroom application 5.8

Ms. Radomsky teaches home economics. Whenever her students have to prepare a recipe, she displays on the whiteboard the following measurements:

Math by the Spoon:

— 3 teaspoons = 1 tablespoon
— 4 tablespoons = 1/4 cup
— 5 tablespoons + 1 teaspoon = 1/3 cup
— 8 tablespoons = 1/2 cup
— 10 tablespoons + 2 teaspoons = 2/3 cup
— 12 tablespoons = 3/4 cup
— 16 tablespoons = 1 cup

More Conversions:

— 1 tablespoon = 1/2 fluid ounce
— 1 cup = 1/2 pint = 8 fluid ounces
— 2 cups = 1 pint = 16 fluid ounces
— 4 cups = 2 pints = 1 quart = 32 fluid ounces
— 16 cups = 4 pints = 1 gallon = 128 fluid ounces

This way her students will not have to overload their working memories by thinking about the conversions during the cooking process but can refer to them, as necessary.

MEANINGFUL MATERIALS

Original learning can be improved if teachers use *meaningful materials*—those to which the students can relate, are connected to their lives, and are more concrete. "Instructional materials affect student achievement as much as any key factor, including effective teaching" (Gewertz, 2012).

Teachers can make original learning more meaningful and vivid by using *primary sources* whenever possible. Document-based questions (DBQs) provide one type of original source. Though these documents are frequently used for assessment, they can also be used to learn or enhance new content.

Examine the following original documents, Rural Americans Move to the Cities, from "Work, Culture and Society in Industrial America." Note how these documents make the study of this era more alive and meaningful to students. Note also how the assessment (essay with corresponding rubric) is used at the end of the documents (Figure 5.2)

■ ■ ■

Teaching With Documents | edteck.com/dbq

Rural Americans Move to the Cities

This question is designed to test your ability to work with historical documents and is based on the accompanying documents 1 – 7. Some of the documents have been edited for the purposes of the question. As you analyze each document, take into account both the sources of the document and the point of view that may be presented in the document.

Directions: This document–based question consists of two parts. In Part A, you are to read each document and answer the question or questions that follow it. In part B, you are to write an essay based on the information in the document and your knowledge of United States history.

Historic Context:
After the Civil War, the United States economy expanded rapidly. Because large cities were centers of intense economic activity, people looking for work converged on them. The need for labor was so great that not only men, but also large numbers of young, unmarried women entered the work force.

This transformation depended not only upon the factory system and a labor force centralized in cities, but also on new technologies, improvement in communications and modern financial systems. Thousands of rural Americans moved to cities as the economy shifted from an agricultural to an industrial base.

Task:
Using information from the documents provided and your knowledge of United States history, write a well-organized essay in which you:

Discuss the reasons why rural Americans moved to the cities in the years between the Civil War and WWI. Include in your discussion what advantages and disadvantages such a move brought them.

Part A:

Directions: Analyze the documents and answer the question or questions that follow each document in the space provided. Your answers will help you write the essay.

Document 1: An excerpt from Russell Conwell's *Acres of Diamonds* 1870.

Baptist minister and founder of Temple University, Russell Conwell first delivered his sermon-lecture "Acres of Diamonds" in 1861 as an eighteen-year-old boy. The message was so well-received that he delivered it some 6,000 times over the next fifty years and received more than $8 million in proceeds including royalties on the printed version.

> The opportunity to get rich, to attain great wealth is here…now within the reach of almost every man and woman…. You have no right to be poor. It is your duty to be rich…. I sympathize with the poor, but the number of poor who are to be sympathized with is very small… let us remember, there is not a poor person in the United States who was not made poor by his own shortcomings…

1. According to Russell Conwell, what was the primary cause of poverty?

Document 2: Chicago World's Fair 1893.

The World's Columbian Exposition, held in Chicago in 1893, was the last and the greatest of the nineteenth century's World's Fairs - a showcase for technology, progress, consumer culture and life in modern America. The Fair was immensely popular and drew over 27 million visitors.

The Ferris Wheel was an engineering marvel and Chicago's answer to the Eiffel Tower, built a few years earlier.

Pittsburgh bridge builder George W. Ferris created the wheel. Its 45-foot axle was the largest single piece of forged steel at the time in the world. The wheel had a diameter of 250 feet and 36 wooden cars that could each hold 60 people.

For 50 cents, people were treated to a 20-minute ride and spectacular view of the fair and Chicago.

View of the fair from the top of the Ferris Wheel

2. Describe how a rural visitor to the Chicago World's Fair might feel about life in the city?

TEACHING WITH DOCUMENTS | EDTECK.COM/DBQ

Document 3: Excerpt from a life history by Harry Reece.

Harry Reece grew up on a farm in Illinois during the late 1800s. In the following narrative, he recalls a trip to the city of Chicago - "the big town" - in the 1890's, and his first experience with the electric trolley. This history is one of a series of interviews that were written by the staff of the Folklore Project of the Federal Writers' Project in 1938.

"I was born in the middle west. Out in the state of Illinois...and it was quite a while before the Chicago World's Fair of 1893. We lived on a farm, and even telephones were curiosities to myself and the country boys of my age. Electric lights were something to marvel at...the old Edison phonograph with its wax cylinder records and earphones was positively ghostly...and trolley cars, well they too were past understanding!

Speaking of trolley cars reminds me of a trip to the 'city' once when I was about a dozen years old. My father and a neighbor, Old Uncle Bill Brandon, had to go up to the Big Town, which was Chicago, on some sort of business...and I suppose I'd been extra diligent at doing chores, weeding potatoes, killing worms on the tomato plants, or something...and Father rewarded me by taking me along.

You can imagine what a time I had seeing things I'd never seen before, in fact had only dreamed about or heard about. When I saw my first trolley car slipping along Cottage Grove Avenue in Chicago...slipping along without horses or engine or apparent motive power...well it was just too darned much for me. I didn't know what to think.

Uncle Bill could understand horses, hogs and cattle, steam engines, army mules and rowboats, and such thing--but that trolley car, with the little spinning wheel at the end of the pole, spinning along against the electric wire above it; was too much for him. Still, he didn't want to confess 'that there was any doggone thing on earth that he couldn't figure out!

I wasn't so anxious to conceal my own ignorance, so with legitimate curiosity asked my Father and Uncle Bill what made the thing go. My Father was a thoughtful man, and before answering studied for a moment. Uncle Bill was more spontaneous. Gosh a'mighty, can't you see what makes her go?' he exclaimed, 'It's that danged rod stickin' up out of the top of her. People's gettin' so cussed smart these days all they need to do to run a street car is to got a fish-pole and stick it up out of the roof of her!"

3a. How does Harry Reece's group respond to the trolley car they saw in Chicago?

3b. What was his response to some of the other new technologies of the era?

Document 4: Laundry in a tenement yard: Park Ave and 107th St.
New York. 1900. Photo taken from an elevated railroad track.

4. By 1900, many rural American found themselves living in city tenement apartments. How does this photograph depict the changes they found in the city?

Document 5: "New Economy Chief Cream Separator" – From Sears Catalogue, 1908. This machine was marketed to farmers and it was used to separate cream from cow's milk.

5. How would the introduction of laborsaving devices impact life in rural America?

TEACHING WITH DOCUMENTS | EDTECK.COM/DBQ

Document 6: Excerpt from *Sister Carrie by Theodore Dreiser, 1900*

Theodore Dreiser was a journalist before he became a novelist; he published Sister Carrie in 1900. It has come to be regarded as an American classic and many consider it the first "modern" American novel. Through its characters and their story, it illustrates the effects of the changing economic structure on American culture. *Sister Carrie* tells the story of eighteen-year-old Carrie Meeber who leaves her small town, drawn to the excitement of promise of the Chicago. She is one of thousands of wage seekers converging on Chicago during the economic boom that followed the Civil War. This passage describes Carrie's first day of work at a shoe factory.

"Carrie at last could scarcely sit still. Her legs began to tire and she wanted to get up and stretch. Would noon never come? It seemed as if she had worked an entire day. She was not hungry at all, but weak, and her eyes were tired, straining at the one point where the eye-punch came down. The girl at the right noticed her squirmings and felt sorry for her. She was concentrating herself too thoroughly--what she did really required less mental and physical strain. There was nothing to be done, however. The halves of the uppers came piling steadily down. Her hands began to ache at the wrists and then in the fingers, and towards the last she seemed one mass of dull, complaining muscles, fixed in an eternal position and performing a single mechanical movement, which became more and more distasteful, until as last it was absolutely nauseating. ….

The place smelled of the oil of the machines and the new leather-- a combination which, added to the stale odors of the building, was not pleasant even in cold weather. The floor, though regularly swept every evening, presented a littered surface. Not the slightest provision had been made for the comfort of the employees, the idea being that something was gained by giving them as little and making the work as hard as possible. What we know of foot-rests, swivel-back chairs, dining-rooms for the girls, clean aprons and curling irons supplied free, and a decent cloak room, were unthought of. The washrooms were disagreeable, crude, if not foul places, and the whole atmosphere was sordid. ….

Carrie said nothing, but bent over her work. She felt as though she could hardly endure such a life. Her idea of work had been so entirely different. All during the long afternoon she thought of the city outside and its imposing show, crowds, and fine buildings. The Chicago World's Fair and the better side of her home life came back. By three o'clock she was sure it must be six, and by four it seemed as if they had forgotten to note the hour and were letting all work overtime. The foreman became a true ogre, prowling constantly about, keeping her tied down to her miserable task. What she heard of the conversation about her only made her feel sure that she did not want to make friends with any of these. When six o'clock came she hurried eagerly away, her arms aching and her limbs stiff from sitting in one position. "

6. Describe the working conditions that Carrie experienced at her first day of work.

Document 7: Statistics on Urban Growth

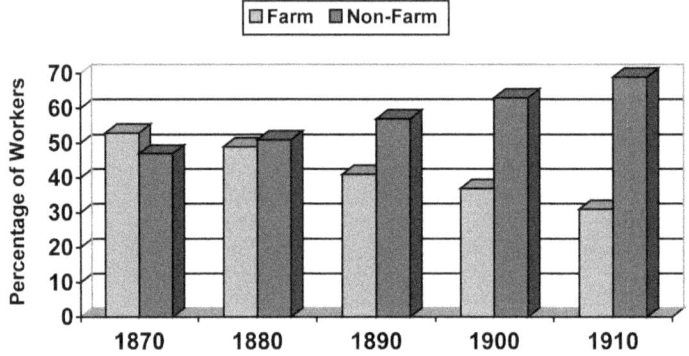

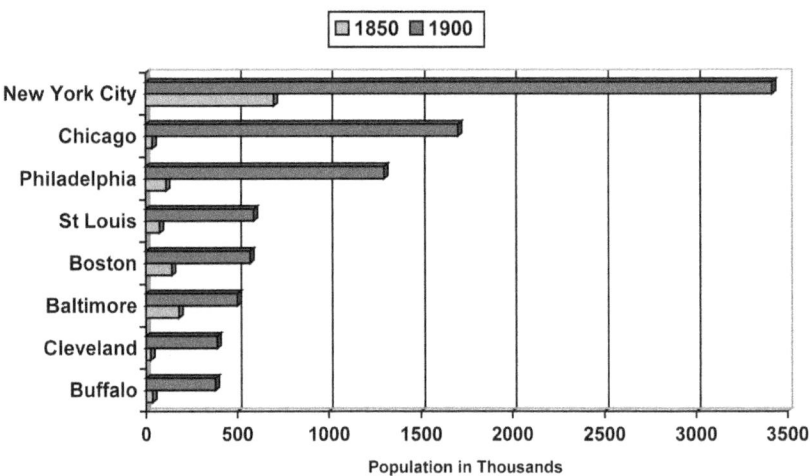

7. Identify two population trends indicated by these graphs.

TEACHING WITH DOCUMENTS | EDTECK.COM/DBQ

Part B Directions:
Using information from the documents provided and your knowledge of United States history, write a well-organized essay that includes an introduction, several paragraphs and a conclusion.

Historic Context:
After the Civil War, the United States economy expanded rapidly. Because large cities were centers of intense economic activity, people looking for work converged on them. The need for labor was so great that not only men, but also large numbers of young, unmarried women entered the work force.

This transformation depended not only upon the factory system and a labor force centralized in cities, but also on new technologies, improvement in communications and modern financial systems. Thousands of rural Americans moved to cities as the economy shifted from an agricultural to an industrial base.

Task:
Using information from the documents provided and your knowledge of United States history, write a well-organized essay in which you:

Discuss the reasons why rural Americans moved to the cities in the years between the Civil War and WWI. Include in your discussion what advantages and disadvantages such a move brought them.

Be sure to:
1. Address all parts of the task by analyzing and interpreting at least 4 documents.
2. Incorporate information from the documents in the body of the essay.
3. Incorporate relevant information throughout the essay.
4. Support the theme with relevant facts and examples.
5. Write a well-developed essay that consistently demonstrates a logical and clear plan of organization.
6. Introduce the theme by establishing a framework beyond a simple restatement of the task or historical context, and conclude the essay with a summation of the theme.

Document-Based Question - Essay Scoring Rubric

5
- Thoroughly addresses all aspects of the *Task* by accurately analyzing and interpreting at least four documents Incorporates information from the documents in the body of the essay
- Incorporates relevant outside information
- Richly supports the theme or problem with relevant facts, examples, and details
- Is a well-developed essay, consistently demonstrating a logical and clear plan of organization
- Introduces the theme or problem by establishing a framework that is beyond a simple restatement of the *Task* or *Historical Context* and concludes with a summation of the theme or problem

4
- Addresses all aspects of the *Task* by accurately analyzing and interpreting at least four documents
- Incorporates information from the documents in the body of the essay
- Incorporates relevant outside information
- Includes relevant facts, examples, and details, but discussion may be more descriptive than analytical
- Is a well-developed essay, demonstrating a logical and clear plan of organization
- Introduces the theme or problem by establishing a framework that is beyond a simple restatement of the *Task* or *Historical Context* and concludes with a summation of the theme or problem

3
- Addresses most aspects of the *Task* or *Historical Context* and concludes by simply repeating the theme or problem or addresses all aspects of the *Task* in a limited way, using some of the documents
- Incorporates some information from the documents in the body of the essay
- Incorporates limited or no relevant outside information
- Includes some facts, examples, and details, but discussion is more descriptive than analytical
- Is a satisfactorily developed essay, demonstrating a general plan of organization
- Introduces the theme or problem by repeating

2
- Attempts to address some aspects of the *Task*, making limited use of the documents
- Presents no relevant outside information
- Includes few facts, examples, and details; discussion restates contents of the documents
- Is a poorly organized essay, lacking focus
- Fails to introduce or summarize the theme or problem

1
- Shows limited understanding of the *Task* with vague, unclear references to the documents
- Presents no relevant outside information
- Includes little or no accurate or relevant facts, details, or examples
- Attempts to complete the *Task*, but demonstrates a major weakness in organization
  Fails to introduce or summarize the theme or problem

0
- Fails to address the *Task*, is illegible, or is a blank paper

Figure 5.2 Work, Culture and Society in Industrial America
(Source: From: "Work, Culture and Society in Industrial America," http://peterpappas.com/journals/industry.htm by Peter Pappas, Reprinted with permission, http://peterpappas.com.)

A word of caution must be introduced here. In using any materials or planning any activity such as a field trip or video, it is imperative that you preview the materials or activity. Not doing so could be disastrous.

Consider this assignment given by a sixth-grade English teacher who wanted to implement the Common Core by selecting biographies of famous people as complex texts. She distributed a sheet with the following directions:

> Discuss his/her early life.
> What challenges did he or she face?
> What were the turning points in his or her life?
> Discuss some fascinating fun facts.
> What was his or her legacy?

The student was to write answers to these questions after reading the selected biography. The teacher displayed biographical books for students to select for the assignment. One boy selected the biography of King Tut. However, when it came to implementing the task, the boy could not complete answers to three of the questions because King Tut died at age 17. When the boy wrote answers only to the questions that were possible, he received a D+. This situation could have been avoided if the teacher had ensured that *all* books she had available for the students to use met the criteria for completing the assignment.

LINKING CONTENT

Original learning becomes more meaningful when subjects are linked together. When studied at the same time rather than in isolation, these subjects are processed with deeper understanding.

Classroom application 5.9

When teaching poetry, Ms. Holland always links the poetry with the music and history of the time in which the poetry was written. She finds that doing this gives the students a better context for the poems, thus making them more meaningful.

Classroom application 5.10

To make what his students formerly considered "dry" topics more meaningful, Mr. Blake connects two goals, one from history and one from economics, in his social studies unit. "Understand developments in foreign policy and domestic politics between the Nixon and Clinton presidencies" is studied with "Understand how gross domestic product (GDP) and inflation and deflation provide indications of the state of the economy." He decided upon these goals after researching topics in both the Common Core State Standards and in Content Knowledge by Kendall and Marzano (1997, p. 489).

Classroom application 5.11

Ms. Pfaff likes to use themes to organize content because they deal with big questions, big ideas, and broader issues. Problems and questions stemming from her themes are examined and solved using the content from several subjects. Some of the themes she used included: Terrorism, Technology, The Aging Population, and Preparing for Hurricanes.

When teaching The Aging Population, she was able to integrate science, history, economics, and politics to solving problems this population causes. The fact that science is helping people live longer has implications for the quality of life, social security, prescription drugs, the federal budget, nursing homes, health care in general, and a myriad of other issues.

After studying The Aging Population, her class explored the political, scientific, social, economic, historical, and geographic implications of Hurricane Sandy.

Classroom application 5.12

Ms. Davidson tries to avoid narrow CCSS content. She has made it a point to examine the standards for her grade level in www.corestandards.org. After looking over several choices, she noted that The Circulatory System (English Language Arts [ELA], grades four and five) could be studied with literature that explains this system, *The Amazing Circulatory System* by John Burstein. She can use this book to apply the ELA standard, "Cite textual evidence to support analysis of what the text says explicitly as well as inferences drawn from the text."

After teaching The Circulatory System along with corresponding literature, Ms. Davidson decides to have her students study two Common Core standards from different but related areas of the *same* subject. She selects The Respiratory System and Taking Care of Your Body.

TRANSFER OF LEARNING

Brain research has verified that elaborate rehearsal and "hands-on" activities are necessary for most learning and that studying a subject in isolation does not readily allow for the transfer of learning from one situation to another (Jensen, 1998). Problem-based learning (sometimes called project-based learning) is highly effective in connecting subjects together.

The underlying idea in problem-based learning is that the goal of education is not to have students do well in school, but to have them do well outside of school. Therefore, students are presented with a real problem, an **authentic problem** that is meaningful to them. The problem should be challenging—one that adults wrestle with in the real world. If the problem is not authentic, does not actually affect the students personally or socially, it should at least be engaging. The best problems are current. The problem may be one offered by the teacher or one suggested by the students. There may be a single solution to the problem or varied solutions, but the solution(s) must be genuine. The problem takes an extended time to complete, usually several weeks.

Once the problem is defined, it becomes the focus of instruction. Goals follow from the problem. Students learn different problem-solving skills. These may be the **scientific method**, or a modified version, depending on the nature of the problem. You may remember that the scientific method has several important steps.

- The problem is specified and students must understand all the terms in the problem before they can go on.
- Tentative guesses (hypotheses) are offered to solve the problem.
- Each hypothesis is individually tested by gathering data.
- Each hypothesis is retested to check results.
- On the basis of hypothesis-testing results, one or several hypotheses are selected to solve the problem.
- The solution is then implemented.
- The solution is monitored to see if it is producing the desired results.
- If not, the above process is repeated until the problem is solved.

In order to test each hypothesis, data must be collected from several different subject areas, allowing students the opportunity to integrate knowledge from different disciplines. The students engage in a collaborative effort to collect and analyze data and select solutions.

Collaboration itself is an important out-of-school mental activity with the problem providing a context for thinking (Resnick, 1987). Working together is also more motivational and develops social skills. Students may work in pairs or in another small-group arrangement. As they work together, they share ideas, discuss solutions, use real, concrete objects such as computers, calculators, or scales. The nature of the activities allows the students to construct their own meaning regarding real-world phenomena (Cole, 2012). The *process* in which students are engaged is as important as the solution.

When a solution is offered by a group, they must go beyond communicating this solution in the traditional forms such as reports, dioramas, or collages. Students must produce **authentic products** to demonstrate what they have learned and how the problem was solved. Exhibits, videos, models, mock-ups, pamphlets, brochures, and computer programs are some examples of products the students can create. The products are then shared with the other groups who may have come up with different solutions.

The teacher's role is most critical in determining the success of problem-based instruction. He or she serves as a coach and a model for the problem-solving skills his or her students will need (Stepien, Johnson, & Checkley, 1997). The teacher must ensure that students believe that they can solve the problem, have enough competence to do so, and can relate their success to *effort*. Attitudinal and verbal communication of the teacher is encouraging, and keeps the students' attention on the process involved in solving the problem as well as in developing the end product.

Of equal importance is setting up a structure in the classroom that will ensure success. This structure necessitates that the teacher provides access to materials to assist the students in the investigating, monitors the interaction between or among students, and encourages students to think for themselves and express their points of view. The teacher must be able to manage logistical and organizational problems in order to ensure that work flows smoothly. Where will materials be stored? How can the environment where many different groups are working on different tasks be controlled? What types of arrangements must be made for out-of-class research the students must conduct in the school library, or with resource people or places within the community itself? If one or several groups finish early, what should be done to keep them involved until the other groups complete their work?

It should be pointed out that though there are many positive characteristics of problem-based learning, there are also several concerns. Given the organizational school structures and prevalent time for meeting the Common Core State Standards, problem-based learning is a difficult strategy to implement.

The strategy needs the support of library and technological resources, which can be expensive. Only a limited amount of information can be covered using this approach. Grading of students' work is a persistent issue. And finally, the teacher must have the knowledge to be able to draw from many different disciplines and the managerial skills to keep the students on target.

However, many educators believe so deeply in problem-based learning that some schools are working on ways to shift instruction from teacher-directed to problem (inquiry)-based learning when implementing the Common Core State Standards (Isselhardt, 2013). These schools are also focusing on the development of alternative pedagogies as well as identification of resources. The Smithsonian is also helping to foster problem-based learning by launching a digital badge program to aid students and teachers in exploring their interests and ideas (Hudson, 2013).

Classroom application 5.13

Ms. Haines wanted to prepare a traditional unit for an upcoming presidential election for her 9th graders but opted for problem-based learning instead. How Can We Make the Best-Informed Choice for President? was the stated problem. Students had the option of selecting one of several topics: researching political parties; researching the nomination process; studying the effect of third-party candidates on prior elections; examining the history of the Constitution on voting; studying demographics and voting; checking backgrounds of the candidates; analyzing personal or personality characteristics of candidates that influence voters; identifying issues the candidates stood for; studying the process of registering to vote; and any other relevant topic suggested by students. They could work in groups of three with specific assignments for *each* group member. If several groups wanted the same topic, they could negotiate.

Before the research began, Ms. Haines explained the scientific method for problem solving; provided practices in the scientific method; assisted each student in deciding what contribution he or she would make in helping solve the problem; provided adequate materials and resources; explained how the materials and resources could be used; established a system for storing materials; and assisted students in selecting partners or small groups. During the process Ms. Haines encouraged students to discuss and explore, and express their ideas; kept students focused on work; and assisted them in determining suitable final products and in sharing their projects in class.

After the research, students could choose from several authentic products to share their knowledge with classmates: prepare pamphlets for the candidates; participate in a debate where they would have to be the candidate they would *not* personally choose for president; write editorials supporting one of the candidates; develop a questionnaire for the community to determine how well versed the local citizens were on the issues, distribute the questionnaire, and collect and analyze the data; design TV commercials supporting candidates; perform fact checks on TV commercials prepared by the actual candidates, or suggest products of their own.

At the end of the project, there would be a mock election in the class.

PATTERNS

Original learning is processed more effectively if the brain sees a *pattern* (Laster, 2007).

Classroom application 5.14

Ms. Glick displays the following equations for the students to observe.

$5 \times 1 = 5$
$5 \times 10 = 50$
$5 \times 100 = 500$
$5 \times 1000 = 5,000$
$5 \times 10,000 = 50,000$
$50 \times 1000 = 50,000$
$500 \times 1000 = 500,000$
$5000 \times 10 = 50,000$
$5,000,000 \times 100,000 = ?$

She asks if the students see a pattern between the factors and their products in all the equations. If so, they can find the answer to the last problem without calculating.

After a few moments the students say that the product contains the same amount of zeroes as there are in the factors. They also state that the when you multiply any factor (multiplicand) by multipliers of 10, 100, 1000, 10,000, etc., you end up with that factor and the number of zeroes in the multiplier. These patterns make it easy to remember how to calculate and check results.

Classroom application 5.15

Ms. Grant teaches general music. She wants her students to understand rhythm. She explains that rhythm in music is constructed on a framework of patterns that center on the meter of the subject piece.

Meter in any piece of music is identified by a fraction. The numerator of the fraction tells the number of beats in a measure. The denominator tells the kind of note that gets one beat. That fundamental pattern can be the foundation upon which a composer builds any combination of rhythms. The fraction 3/4 would indicate that there will be three beats in a measure and that a quarter note (which is what the 4 in 3/4 stands for) gets one beat.

In a basic 3/4 meter, the fundamental framework consists of three beats per measure repeated throughout the section. Those three beats usually follow an accent pattern where the first beat of each measure is the strongest, and the second and third beats are weaker. The resulting pattern would be strong-weak-weak, strong-weak-weak. Ms. Grant has her students tap that pattern on their desks with their left hand beating the strong accent and the right hand beating the two weaker ones. To follow up with an example, Ms. Grant plays the waltz from *The Merry Widow* on the piano, emphasizing the meter. She then replays part of the waltz, this time having the students tapping the meter.

Ms. Grant repeats the exercise using a 2/4 meter where there are two beats in a measure with the first beat the stronger and the second beat the weaker. Strong-weak, strong-weak is the pattern. Ms. Grant has her students tap that meter on their desks with the accent on the left hand, the first beat of the measure the stronger beat, and the right hand the weaker second beat. Ms. Grant then plays a Sousa march with which the students are familiar, "The Stars and Stripes Forever," emphasizing the meter. She replays part of the march, this time having the students tapping the meter.

The next day Ms. Grant plays recordings of random pieces that are waltzes (3/4 meters) or marches (2/4 meters) to see if her students can differentiate between the two different meters.

When Ms. Grant is confident that her students understand how the two basic meters she has introduced are built, she refers them to the website http://musescore.org, where they click on Notation. There they can explore other meters. She encourages students who want to have a deeper understanding of meter to find friendly websites that offer more examples of different meters and share these websites with classmates. For budding composers, Ms. Grant leads those interested students to the music-writing program, Sibelius.

Classroom application 5.16

Ms. Kingsley wants her first graders to understand mathematical patterns in order to understand and remember addition facts. Using manipulatives, her students have already learned the commutative property of addition, namely, that two numbers can be added in any order (change their places) and get the same results. Continuing to use manipulatives, the students learn that subtraction undoes addition. Therefore, if they know one addition fact, they actually know four, and these four facts form a number family.

For example,

$2 + 3 = 5 / 3 + 2 = 5$ The commutative law
$5 - 2 = 3 / 5 - 3 = 2$ Subtraction undoes addition

When Ms. Kingsley is confident that her students have a firm foundation with this pattern, she introduces them to $485 + 387 = 872$ and challenges them for three more facts related to this problem that would make up the number family. Even though they cannot yet perform operations with three-digit numerals, her students can use the pattern to get the correct answer.

Many are able to write the remaining three equations in the number family:

387 + 485 = 872
872 − 485 = 387
872 − 387 = 485

When they do succeed, Ms. Kingsley tells her first graders how proud she is of them because they can work with such big numbers, those that students in the *third grade* use. Then she asks them to come up with their own big addition number equation and see if their classmates can find the pattern in it and make a family out of that equation.

NARRATIVES

Original content can be enhanced when *narratives* are used instead of or in addition to textbooks.

Classroom application 5.17

Mr. Holt is teaching a unit on the Civil War in his seventh-grade United States history class. When his students were close to completing the unit, he gave them a choice of reading *The Red Badge of Courage*, or *Killing Lincoln*. Students were to list examples of what they learned in the readings that made the unit more relevant and meaningful. The students formed groups to share their insights.

Classroom application 5.18

Ms. Mason is a biology teacher. In addition to the biology text, Ms. Mason has her students read and discuss *The Immortal Life of Henrietta Lacks*.

ACTIVE INVOLVEMENT/USE OF SENSES

Active involvement and use of senses make original learning more easily and accurately processed. Hands-on activities are particularly effective because neuroscientists have confirmed that the hands are the organs of the brain (Jensen, 1998).

Classroom application 5.19

Ms. Henry recalled how she learned the differences among cups, pints, and quarts. She was handed a worksheet that stated the relationships on the top and then was asked to complete a list of problems applying these relationships. Ms. Henry knew that teaching the content this way was too abstract, even for her higher achievers.

She set up several work tables which displayed measuring cups able to hold cups, pints, and quarts; a large pitcher of *colored* water; and containers (milk cartons, cream cartons, and jars of different sizes) that represented cups, pints, and quarts. On each table she placed an activity card. Ms. Henry formed groups for each table. Each group was to complete the activities in the order designated by the activity cards.

Ms. Henry explained the directions and had several students repeat them. The directions were as follows:

> Find the smallest containers.
> Read the label and tell how much liquid those containers hold.
> Find the next smallest containers.
> Read the label and tell how much liquid those next smallest containers hold.
> Which containers are left? Read their labels and tell how much liquid they hold.
> Take a measuring cup and fill it with colored water up to one cup. How many of those cups do you need to fill the pint measuring cup? How many of those cups do you need to fill the quart measuring cup?
> Take a measuring cup and fill it with colored water up to one pint. How many of those pints do you need to fill the quart measuring cup?

DISCOVERY

Original learning is best processed if students can *discover* relationships for themselves. Discovery learning is more efficient.

Try the following: Write the **first answer** that comes to mind to the question, "What is the formula for the circumference of a circle?" Stop reading and write your answer now.

It is highly likely that you wrote $C = \pi r^2$, and if you did, it should tell you that you do not know the difference between linear and surface measurement. This is probably NOT your fault. Think of how you likely learned about circumference. Was it more like the way it was presented by Mr. Kravitt or by Mr. Pastor?

Classroom application 5.20

> Mr. Kravitt: Today we are going to learn how to find the circumference of a circle. The circumference is the distance around the circle. The formula for the circumference of a circle is $C = \pi d$. [He writes this formula on the board.] Open your books to page 73 and let's do the first problem.

This problem is followed by several more problems performed in class, some providing the length of the radius instead of the diameter. Additional problems are assigned for homework. The next day Mr. Kravitt checks the homework and moves on to the perimeter of a different plane figure.

If you "learned" the formula for the circumference of a circle the way it was presented by Mr. Kravitt, it is probable that you forgot the formula because you learned it by rote and it had little meaning for you. "Learning" as exemplified in Classroom application 5.20 is not meaningful and should be avoided.

Now consider the presentation of Mr. Pastor.

Classroom application 5.21

> Mr. Pastor: Today we are going to discover the formula for the circumference of a circle. What does circumference mean? [Pause] Frank.
>
> Frank: The distance around a circle.
>
> Mr. Pastor: Good, Frank. [Mr. Pastor writes the definition on the board and then distributes to everyone in the class a packet containing different-sized colored circles, a tape measure, and a structured chart. He encourages students to place any personal items with circular shapes they may have on the desk.] Now measure the circumference and diameter of each circle I gave you and some of your own circular objects and write the measurements on the chart in your packet. [He has already reproduced the chart on a whiteboard in the front of the room.] (Table 5.2).
>
> **Table 5.2 Circumference of a Circle**
>
> | CIRCUMFERENCE | DIAMETER |
> | --- | --- |
> | | |
>
> Mr. Pastor: [When all students have completed the measurements, he asks five of the students to each place one of their results on the whiteboard.] Take a few moments to see if you can find a pattern in the measurements regardless of the circle sizes. [Pause] Jeanette.
>
> Jeanette: The diameter is roughly one third the size of the circumference.

Mr. Pastor: Excellent, Jeanette. Can anyone state that in another way? [Pause] Paul.

Paul: I was thinking the circumference is three times the diameter.

Mr. Pastor: Exactly three times in all the examples, Paul?

Paul: Uh, uh, no, it's, it's almost or approximately three times.

Mr. Pastor: Let's see if Paul is right. Check the measurements of all your circles and personal objects to see if they all follow the same pattern. [After the students check the measurements and decide that all the circles follow the same pattern, Mr. Pastor writes on the whiteboard: The circumference of a circle is approximately three times its diameter.] So you were right, Paul. There is a mathematical name for something that means approximately but not exactly three times, and that is the Greek letter pi (π). It is the irrational number 3.1416 . . . or 22/7. You've just reviewed irrational numbers, so who can remind us of what they are? [Pause] Elly.

Elly: One that can't be expressed as a decimal with a repeating pattern, and can't be expressed as the quotient of two integers.

Mr. Pastor: Great memory, Elly. Do 3.1416 . . . and 22/7 meet those criteria? [Elly and the rest of the students think for a moment then nod in agreement.] If the circumference is approximately three times the diameter, no matter how large or small the circle, how can this sentence on the board be expressed in terms of π? [Pause] Jim.

Jim: Circumference is π times d.

Mr. Pastor: How can π times d be expressed mathematically, Jim?

Jim: π times d or πd.

[Mr. Pastor writes under the sentence defining circumference he has already written on the whiteboard, the equation $C = \pi \times d = \pi d$.]

Mr. Pastor: O.K., Jim, what is the relationship between the diameter and the radius of a circle?

Jim: The diameter's twice the radius or 2r.

Mr. Pastor: Since the diameter is twice the radius, Jim, how can we express the formula in terms of r?

Jim: [Thinks for a moment] Well d = 2r, that's what I just said, so . . . C = π2r or 2πr.

Mr. Pastor: Excellent. What law allows us to change the order of the three factors in a multiplication problem without changing the product? [Pause] Olga.

Olga: The commutative . . . uh, no, the associative law of multiplication.

Mr. Pastor: Why wouldn't the commutative law be applicable in this case, Olga?

Olga: Because it involves only two factors and we have three.

Mr. Pastor adds C = 2πr next to the circumference equations already written on the whiteboard. He then has one of the students transfer the information to a poster that is displayed in the front of the room for reinforcement and future reference.

By using the discovery approach, Mr. Pastor gives the students a better chance to understand the formula by giving it *meaning*. If they forget the formula, they can reconstruct the experience they had in discovering the formula (measuring the diameters and circumferences of the different circles to find the pattern) to help recall it.

Many teachers complain that discovery takes too much time. However, discovery learning is more efficient in that it leads to understanding (meaning) and therefore long-term retention.

In addition to relationships, discovery can also be used to learn concepts. Consider how actively involved and engaged all students are in the original learning in the following classrooms.

Classroom application 5.22

Ms. Barton tells her class that she has an idea that she wants them to guess. She will give them examples of the idea and non-examples of the idea. They are to compare the examples and contrast them with the non-examples.

Ms. Barton presents several matched pairs that contain examples and non-examples of the idea. Examples are displayed in the Example column, and non-examples are displayed in the Non-example column. The students are to identify the characteristics or attributes of the examples by comparing the examples and contrasting them with the non-examples.

To have her students concentrate on the critical attributes of the examples that represent the concept, Ms. Barton ensures that when she chooses her set of examples, their noncritical attributes are as *different* as possible. This selection allows the students to concentrate on the critical attributes.

When she chooses matched pairs of examples and non-examples, she ensures that their non-critical attributes are as *similar* as possible. This selection allows the students to concentrate on the differences between examples and non-examples.

Ms. Barton offers the following examples and non-examples for her concept:

Examples	Non-examples
salmon	salad
castle	caddy
almond	altar
gnat	not
sword	swing
knowingly	factual
whole	hole

(Note how the noncritical attributes of the examples—words that contain silent letters—are different from each other in initial letters, number of syllables, and parts of speech, and how the example and non-example pairs are similar.) Even though example and non-example sets can be introduced as a single pair first, or all together, Ms. Barton has decided to present all the pairs at once.

Ms. Barton: "What do the examples have that the non-examples do not have?"

Many suggestions by the students might be unanticipated, and the teacher, even if he or she plans the matched pairs carefully, must be armed with or think "on the spot" of additional examples and non-example pairs that will finally elicit the critical attributes of any concept he or she wishes to teach.

Once the essential attributes of a concept are identified, the students basically know the concept. This is true whether or not they have a **label** (name) for the concept. *The name or label is less important than knowing the attributes.* However, eventually the set of attributes has to be labeled.

Remember that knowing the label is not necessarily the same as knowing the concept. Students will often use labels for concepts without having a clear idea of their attributes. A typical example is a kindergarten student who may verbally state the name "six" but cannot count six objects if they are positioned differently. The same student may also count the same object more than once, or skip the object.

Adults often use terms they do not fully understand. Most adults thought that the term "impeach" meant that a president could be thrown out of office instead of that the president would undergo a trial to see if he or she should be removed.

When a student uses a term and you are not sure whether or not s/he really understands it, *ask for an example.* Also ask for a non-example, because in understanding a concept, a student should know *what it is* as well as *what it is not*.

The teacher further determines whether or not the students know the concept by offering *one at a time in random order* different examples and non-examples which the students have to place under the correct column. Students must state *why* they have made their placement choice. The next step is having the students offer their own examples and non-examples and also list them in the proper columns. At this time the students should be able to explain or justify why their offerings are examples or not. In the final step the teacher has the student apply the concept to deepen understanding.

It is more effective to present non-examples that do not all belong to the same category. If "adjective" is the concept to be taught, the teacher should display non-examples that represent various other parts of speech such as verbs; adverbs; conjunctions; pronouns; prepositions; or interjections. Using non-examples from different categories makes it easier to contrast the examples and non-examples so that the critical attributes of the examples stand out.

Examples and non-examples can take many different forms. They can be sentences, as in the next classroom application.

Classroom application 5.23

Mr. Paige is teaching a grammar lesson. He wants his students to understand that they should use the possessive case before gerunds. Gerund is a "foreign" word to his students and to most students and adults. Mr. Paige puts the following list of examples and non-examples on the smartboard.

Examples	Non-examples
Walking is good for you.	You are *walking* too fast.
I like *walking*.	*Walking* away from the accident, Tom shook his head
He won an endurance contest for *walking*	While he was walking, he tripped on a rock.

Mr. Paige highlights the word *walking*, allowing his students to concentrate on the use of that particular word in the sentences. He is prepared to give additional examples and non-examples if his students do not see the differences right away. They read the examples and non-examples in unison, allowing the students to hear the differences.

Finally, they recognize that in the examples, walking is the –ing form of a verb that is used as a noun, not as a participle. (His students have already learned what a participle is.)

When he gives additional sentences containing examples and non-examples, Mr. Paige has his students state if the examples and non-examples in the sentences are gerunds or participles. Correct answers are added to the corresponding Example or Non-example heading on the smartboard. Then Mr. Paige asks the students to make up their own sentences using participles and gerunds and justify why they contain gerunds or participles. He adds the students' sentences on the smartboard under the proper heading.

Examples and non-examples can also be symbols or pictures. If the attributes of Impressionist paintings were to be identified, all the examples would be paintings from that period, and the non-examples would be paintings from *several other* periods.

Classroom application 5.24

Ms. Schultz teaches art history. She wants to introduce to her 10th graders a unit on Impressionist painters. Ms. Schultz exhibited examples and non-examples of works from the following artists:

Examples	Non-examples
Monet	Rembrandt
Pissarro	Vermeer
Sisley	Botticelli
Degas	Da Vinci
Renoir	Caravaggio

After comparing examples of the representative paintings and contrasting the examples with the non-examples, students identified the following attributes of the examples (Impressionists): blurry; no carefully delineated lines; bright, light colors; shadowy; incomplete; seem to capture a moment in time; show everyday scenes; depict regular people not royalty.

As a culminating activity, the class prepared an Impressionist gallery. Each student was assigned to write a brief biography of one Impressionist artist (including dates). This bio was displayed with one representative painting of that artist found on the web with the date of that work. A website was identified by each student for others to gain more information about his or her assigned artist. Then the students lined up the paintings *chronologically* for display and further discussion. Students were able to describe changes in the paintings as the years progressed. Other classes were invited to view the exhibit.

In all of the above discovery approaches, students are actively involved in learning the concepts. Active involvement is an effective information-processing technique, especially when learning original content.

It should be stated that concepts can also be taught using an expository or direct presentation form instead of employing an inductive approach. Using the expository method, the teacher would begin by identifying and defining the concept. Then s/he would provide the critical attributes of the concept and identify examples and non-examples. In the final step, s/he would have the students offer their own examples and non-examples.

Even though the expository approach can be effective, the inductive approach presented earlier, where the students must *discover* the attributes for themselves, gets the students more engaged mentally. Not only will the students learn the concept more efficiently but also they will retain it longer.

TECHNOLOGY

This section could not be concluded without mentioning technology. A thorough discussion of technology would be at minimum a book in itself, but here we will simply touch on the highlights.

When learning original content (and reinforcing that content, Chapter 6), teachers can use technology to keep students actively involved and learning more vivid. Currently, technological resources include camcorders; overhead projectors; TV/VCRs; digital video disk (DVD) players, audio recorders; cameras; computers; and mobile smartphones.

Technology, especially computer technology, should be infused into the curriculum. Computer technology is a valuable resource for research, reinforcement, and enrichment. But as with all resources, it should complement and supplement the teacher's role and help tailor information for each learner's needs. *Technology should not be used for the sake of technology but should be used when it will be effective in implementing goals and objectives.*

Of particular concern for teachers are programs such as PowerPoint, which assists the teacher in preparing materials for overhead presentations, Blackboard Academic Suite, which enables whole courses to be delivered online with constant communication between the students and teacher, and social media applications that allow students and teachers to interact with others anywhere in the world.

Interactive whiteboards (smartboards) are now being used to integrate digital information into teaching. These whiteboards enhance communication and engage students by making it possible for teachers to write notes; list student ideas; insert graphics; link to websites; cut, copy, and paste information from any application for display on the whiteboard; and save work for future use.

In a recent study it was reported that the use of whiteboards did not have any noted impact on children's test scores (Nightingale, 2006). This result may be attributed to the lack of appropriate training for teachers in the use of whiteboards and the fact that this technology allows lessons to flow too quickly without adequate time for developing student understanding. Yet, teachers in the study indicated that whiteboards increased motivation by keeping students engaged in interactive content.

eChalk designed its Online Learning Environment specifically for K–12. It offers a teacher-friendly communication tool that works with existing teaching practices. Among other activities, eChalk allows teachers to save lesson plans, forms, resources, and materials. Students can submit homework, making it easier for teachers to manage assignments electronically. Teachers can share lessons, resources, and syllabi. Communication among all levels of school district personnel is more easily facilitated.

AlphaSmart is currently being seen more frequently in schools. It is a sturdy, portable computer accessory that allows students access to word processing. AlphaSmart shows text using a keyboard with a liquid crystal display (LCD).

The Internet, a network of other networks interconnected to millions of computers in all nations, has enormous potential in and out of the classroom. Besides e-mail, teachers can use mailing lists, discussion groups, chats, newsgroups, social networking sites, and forums to connect electronically with people and resources internationally.

Social media sites such as Facebook make it possible for students and teachers with common interests to interact worldwide. Forums are sections within an online service that provide information on a specific subject. The forum may include a library where various fields can be downloaded and may allow for a conference room.

The Internet's subset, the World Wide Web (WWW), provides for computer content to be accessed through an Internet browser. The WWW makes it possible for a specific website to be easily located and accessed from computers, tablet devices, and mobile smartphones with Internet access. Websites offer a valuable source of information from government, industry, and different organizations that is available within seconds.

In short, teachers can use technology to record lectures and notes; use e-books; keep connected with families; make learning fun; track attendance and behavior; and promote collaboration (Steinberg, 2013). Teachers have also been able to flip their classrooms (Tips to Help You Flip Your Classroom, 2013). Flipping reverses the traditional model of instruction during class with homework after class. In the new model, students watch the teacher's (original) instruction outside of class through videos, and then are involved in follow-up discussions and hands-on activities inside the classroom. Students have control over when and how many times they watch the videos, and may go back and see information repeated before moving on again. This procedure allows students to process and synthesize content more efficiently, thereby allowing subsequent class discussions to be more involved and enriched.

In general, computer technology, with its access to text, sound, graphics, simulation, and video, has the potential to lead students to higher learning levels and engage them in active learning using multiple pathways.

The innovation that has had the most impact in the classroom is the iPad. This device is changing teaching and learning dramatically in schools (Tan, 2013).

Classroom application 5.25

Mr. Franklin's fifth-grade students all have iPads. As a result, when Breanna was reading a passage about harvesting in her e-book, *Esperanza Rising*, she was able to immediately call up the definition of the word *reap*. Mr. Franklin's class no longer has to make class trips to the computer lab to perform academic research. In seconds his students can access facts and images. Instead of having to call on one student at a time, Mr. Franklin's students answer his questions on their iPads. This process allows him to receive instant feedback regarding their knowledge. And time is saved writing homework assignments on the board because students can automatically download and complete assignments on their iPads.

Students own and cherish their cell phones (Nielsen, 2012). So why not capture this medium to engage students in meaningful learning?

Classroom application 5.26

Ms. Dickerson decided to capitalize on the popularity of texting. Whenever her students have to write a draft, she encourages them to first text their thoughts down. This process gives students the impetus to capture, collect, and create elusive ideas. Her students subsequently revise their initial texts so that the final draft is presented in standard English.

Classroom application 5.27

Mr. Waldman teaches eighth-grade English. He has his class members each get a free account on Google Voice. This account enables his students to use their cell phones to store voice messages, sound bites, oral reports, and assignments. It also enables Mr. Waldman to write comments on each clip, share, and post them.

In Mr. Waldman's classroom, students can record oral reports on their cell phones and can continue to rerecord the report until satisfied before sharing it with their classmates. Since most cell phones now can shoot videos, Mr. Waldman has his students video record their and others' speaking skills. The students then view, listen to, and evaluate the recordings. Mr. Waldman first models the evaluation in a positive way to ensure that subsequent student evaluations of each other are constructive and respectful.

Mr. Waldman is also aware of how effective drama is in learning. After reading a scene or chapter in literature, he has his students video themselves on their cell phones, acting out the scene or chapter.

SELF-REFLECTION

- How vivid is the new content you present to your students?
- Think of some lessons you taught recently. What impact do you think they had? How might you have taught the same content to produce a greater impact?
- How have you used hands-on learning in your classes?
- How many senses were your students involved with in your instruction within the past several weeks?
- How actively involved are your students when learning new content?
- When have you offered your students the opportunity to preview new content?
- How have you used contrast to let new content be processed more efficiently?
- How much information are your students allowed to discover for themselves?
- What meaningful materials have you used recently?
- How have you connected content in your instruction?
- Have you tried problem solving in your classroom? If not, have you incorporated authentic problems and authentic products in your assessments?
- What patterns have you presented your students in the content you have taught?
- What narratives have you used to explore and enhance content?
- How do you introduce new concepts?
- When did you last use examples to clarify concepts?
- How do you know that your students know the attributes of concepts?
- How do you make the abstract concrete?
- How tech-savvy are you? If you are not tech-savvy, what do you plan to do about it?
- How will you use the ideas in this chapter in future instruction?

Chapter Six

Strengthening and Deepening New Learning

The forgetting curve tells us that most of original learning is forgotten within the first 24 hours. This information has serious implications for teachers. Once the original learning is processed, it must be reinforced at least once within the first 24 hours. Moreover, it must be subsequently reinforced in at least *four different* ways in order to be retained (Nuthall, 1999).

MODELING

One way learning can be strengthened (reinforced) is by *modeling* the new learning, especially if the learning is a skill (Bright, 2012).

Classroom application 6.1

Mr. Benedict is teaching his chemistry class the correct and safe way to cut glass tubing. He demonstrates the process several times. Then, under his supervision, he has several of his students practice with feedback from him and the other class members.

Classroom application 6.2

Ms. Pinto has taught her class pronouns. She reinforces the content by placing two paragraphs on the whiteboard. The only difference between them is that one contains nouns and the other the pronouns that have replaced their corresponding nouns. Then she goes through the paragraph with the pronouns, identifying and underlining each. As her students identify the pronouns' corresponding nouns, she writes the nouns above their pronouns. When she is confident that her students are

80   Chapter 6

comfortable with the content, she puts another set of paragraphs on the whiteboard and has the students identify both the pronouns and which nouns they represent.

Classroom application 6.3

Ms. Madden is confident that her fourth graders are proficient in their multiplication facts. She is also sure that they know prime numbers, composite numbers, factors, multiples, greatest common factor, least common multiple, and the identity number for division.

She then teaches a lesson on reducing fractions to lowest terms. At the end of the lesson she models the process by performing several examples on the whiteboard while slowly *verbalizing* the process. She wants to ensure that her students cannot only perform the process but understand why it works. Her first modeling example is the fraction 9/12.

Ms. Madden: Let us practice by reducing 9/12 to lowest terms. Hmm, let me see now, the greatest common factor of 9 and 12 is 3. So we can divide both 9 and 12 evenly by 3. We are actually dividing 9/12 by 3/3 because 3/3 is another name for 1. And we know that if we divide any number by 1, we don't change the value of the number because 1 is the identity number for division. 9 divided by 3 is 3 and 12 divided by 3 is 4. Therefore, 9/12 = 3/4.

THE LAW OF DISTRIBUTED PRACTICE

Both teachers and students should understand and apply the law of distributed practice. This law states that short practice periods distributed over a long period of time are more learning efficient than one long practice session (Mumford et al., 1994).

Cramming for exams is a typical example of inefficient learning. Studying a subject a few minutes each day will yield better results than cramming that subject the night before an exam. A student who crams may do well on the exam but will not retain the information as s/he would through shorter review (practice) periods.

The same law applies when learning a skill, whether it is related to sports or to playing a musical instrument. Practicing a piece of music only 10 minutes a day, every day for a week, will lead to greater achievement than practicing an hour once just before the next lesson.

Classroom application 6.4

Ms. Madden has taught her class to reduce fractions to lowest terms (Classroom application 6.3). As a warm-up, for several days she begins her class by giving her students three fractions to reduce to lowest terms.

MEANINGFUL MATERIALS/ACTIVITIES

Learning can be strengthened by using a *meaningful* worksheet (Figure 6.1) at the end of a lesson or for homework.

Note that this worksheet has several meaningful characteristics. There is a brief review of new content at the top which not only reinforces the content for those who already understand it, but serves as a support for those who may need it. There are clear proportional representative symbols of cups, pints, and quarts. Abbreviations are reinforced and subsequently used. Academically weaker students have the opportunity to succeed and more confident students are challenged (1 pint + 1 cup = _____ cups) along with some more demanding questions at the end.

SUMMARIZING

Learning can be strengthened by *summarizing* new content at the end of a lesson.

Classroom application 6.5

Mr. Frank has completed an introductory lesson on mammals. He asks his students to summarize the common characteristics of mammals, especially characteristics that make their class (mammals) different from birds and reptiles. He lists the students' (correct) responses on the board. Students copy these characteristics into their science notebooks.

Frequently, teachers will reinforce learning by summarizing/reviewing the prior day's content briefly at the beginning of the next lesson.

Classroom application 6.6

> Mr. Frank: Yesterday we began to study mammals [Classroom application 6.5]. What did we find that their general characteristics were? [Pause] Latisha.
>
> Latisha: They have hair or fur, nurse their young. Uh, oh yeah, give birth to live young and, and, let me think . . . are warm-blooded.
>
> Mr. Frank: Great, Latisha, and today we will continue to study mammals, especially those that have some different characteristics from those we examined yesterday.

(See application 6.21 for a different perspective on reviewing prior content.)

Name_____

Liquid Measurement

Remember: 2 cups (c.) = 1 pint (pt.)
2 pints (pt.) = 1 quart (qt.)
4 cups (c.) = 1 quart (qt.)

Look at the pictures. Fill in the blanks.

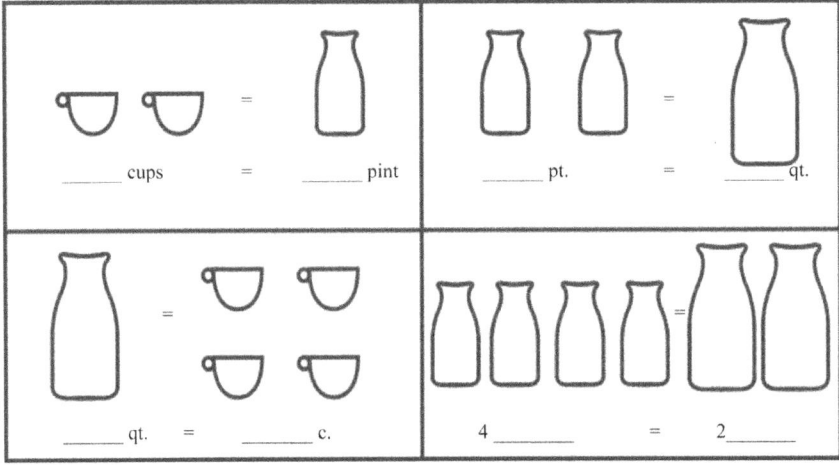

Fill in the blank spaces.

1. 2 c. = _____
2. 2 _____ = 1 qt.
3. 4 c. = _____ qt.
4. 2 cups + 1 cup = _____ cups
5. 1 pint + 1 cup = _____ cups

Optional Challenge (Use abbreviations.)

1. Mrs. Wilson poured 8 cups of tomato juice for her family. Is this more or less than a pint? _____
2. Joan drinks 1 qt. of milk a day. How many pt. would that be? _____
3. Eddie's mother bought 8 pt. of sour cream. How many qt. would that be? _____
4. 1 c. = _____ pt.

Figure 6.1.

There are many other ways to summarize learning, especially when multiple modalities are involved (Wilson, 2006): Students can

- state new content in their own words;
- teach new content to another person and get that person to actually learn the content;
- put the original learning in writing;
- draw a picture, diagram, web, chart of the new learning, whichever is relevant.

Classroom application 6.7

Just before the end of each class, Mr. Graham has his students summarize *in writing* what they have learned. As each student hands in his/her submission, Mr. Graham distributes to each a passport to the next class. This activity has a twofold benefit. Because the students know in advance that they will have to summarize what they learned, they are particularly attentive so that they will have something to write. This activity also gives Mr. Graham the opportunity to determine how much of the content the students have actually learned.

Classroom application 6.8

Ms. Petroff asks her students to draw a mental map, a graphic such as a chart or picture, that makes personal sense to them regarding four of the eight parts of speech they have learned so far (article, noun, adjective, pronoun). Jeremy makes a chart (Figure 6.2) and explains it to the class:

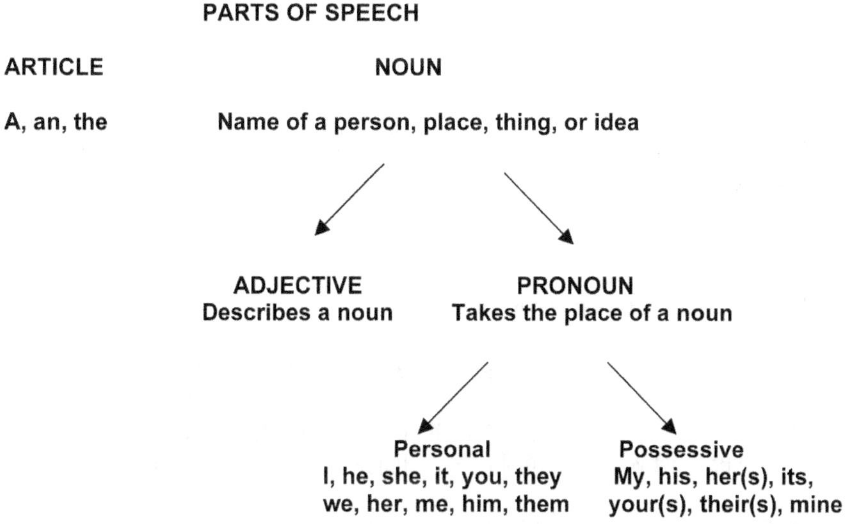

PARTS OF SPEECH

ARTICLE　　　　　　　　　**NOUN**

A, an, the　　　　　　　　　Name of a person, place, thing, or idea

ADJECTIVE　　　　　　　**PRONOUN**
Describes a noun　　　　　Takes the place of a noun

　　　　　　　　　　Personal　　　　　　　　Possessive
　　　　　　　　　　I, he, she, it, you, they　　My, his, her(s), its,
　　　　　　　　　　we, her, me, him, them　　your(s), their(s), mine

Figure 6.2.

VIEWING CONTENT IN NEW WAYS

Content can be reinforced by looking at it in *new* ways.

Classroom application 6.9

Mr. Adams teaches the fourth grade. In this grade students must become proficient in learning their multiplication facts and be able to state them quickly. Rather than having the students recite them by rote, Mr. Adams presents the following multiplication tables on the smartboard and asks the students if they already know any math laws or see any patterns in these tables that will make remembering multiplication facts easier.

Multiplication tables

2 x 1=2	3 x 1=3	4 x 1=4	5 x 1=5	6 x 1=6	7 x 1=7	8 x 1=8	9 x 1=9
2 x 2=4	3 x 2=6	4 x 2=8	5 x 2=10	6 x 2=12	7 x 2=14	8 x 2=16	9 x 2=18
2 x 3=6	3 x 3=9	4 x 3=12	5 x 3=15	6 x 3=18	7 x 3=21	8 x 3=24	9 x 3=27
2 x 4=8	3 x 4=12	4 x 4=16	5 x 4=20	6 x 4=24	7 x 4=28	8 x 4=32	9 x 4=36
2 x 5=10	3 x 5=15	4 x 5=20	5 x 5=25	6 x 5=30	7 x 5=35	8 x 5=40	9 x 5=45
2 x 6=12	3 x 6=18	4 x 6=24	5 x 6=30	6 x 6=36	7 x 6=42	8 x 6=48	9 x 6=54
2 x 7=14	3 x 7=21	4 x 7=28	5 x 7=35	6 x 7=42	7 x 7=49	8 x 7=56	9 x 7=63
2 x 8=16	3 x 8=24	4 x 8=32	5 x 8=40	6 x 8=48	7 x 8=56	8 x 8=64	9 x 8=72
2 x 9=18	3 x 9=27	4 x 9=36	5 x 9=45	6 x 9=54	7 x 9=63	8 x 9=72	9 x 9=81

Mr. Adams: Boys and girls, look across the first row. [He runs his hand across the row.] What pattern do you see here? [Pause] Jeremy.

Jeremy: All those numbers multiply 1.

Mr. Adams: And what is the result, Jeremy?

Jeremy: You end up with the same number you started out with.

Mr. Adams: Excellent, Jeremy. Now think, class, and raise your hand if you can remind us what you know about 1 for multiplication. [Pause] Jessica.

Jessica: 1 is the identity number for multiplication.

Mr. Adams: And what does that mean, Jessica?

Jessica: You can multiply any number by 1 and get the same number.

Mr. Adams: Suppose, Jessica, that instead of multiplying any number by 1 you multiply 1 by any number, what do you get then?

Jessica: The same number.

Mr. Adams: Right, and what law lets us switch places in multiplication and get the same number? [Pause] Hector.

Hector: The commutative law.

Mr. Adams: Good thinking, Hector. Now class, look at the rest of the table. Where else do you see the commutative law? [Pause] Janet.

Janet: 4 x 6 and 6 x 4, 7 x 8 and 8 x 7 . . . in a lot of places.

Mr. Adams: Right, so that if you know one multiplication fact, you know two. And if you think about that, by the time you get to the nine table, how many new facts do you have to memorize if you know the commutative law, Janet?

Janet: [Thinks for a while.] Only one.

Mr. Adams: And which one is that?

Janet: 9 x 9.

Mr. Adams: See, if you know the commutative law, it saves you a lot of trouble. Next I want you all to look specifically at the 2 table. What do you notice about that table? [Pause] Matt.

Matt: All the answers are even.

Mr. Adams: What else?

Matt: They all differ by two.

Mr. Adams: What is multiplication, Matt?

Matt: Repeated addition.

Mr. Adams: What does 2 x 4 mean?

Matt: 4 added 2 times.

Mr. Adams: So if you forget what 2 times 4 is, how else can you find the answer?

Matt: Add 4 and 4.

Mr. Adams: You understand that well, Matt. Now class, what is special about the 5 table? [Pause] Denise.

Denise: The answers all end in 5 or 0.

Mr. Adams: Super. I want everyone to look at the products in the 9 table. See if you can identify any pattern. [Pause] Michael.

Michael: Like all tables they differ by the table, in this case 9.

Mr. Adams: That's right but there is something very special about the products in the 9 table. Look at them very carefully and see if you can find the pattern.

[Students look but no one can find the pattern.]

Mr. Adams: 9 x 2=18. When you add the digits in 18, what do you get? Michael.

Michael: 9.

Mr. Adams: 9 x 3=27. When you add the digits in 27, what do you get, Michael?

Michael: 9 again.

Mr. Adams: Look at all the products in the 9 table. Do they all follow the same pattern?

Michael: Yeah. Their digits all add up to 9. That's real cool.

Mr. Adams: It's a great way to check if your multiplication by nine is correct. If you multiply a number by 9 and end up with a product that is 28, could that product be right?

Michael: No.

Mr. Adams: So let us summarize all the patterns we just discovered to help you remember multiplication facts.

Strengthening and Deepening New Learning 87

GAMES

Students can reinforce learning by *designing* a game that shows that both the game creator and its participants know the new learning.

Classroom application 6.10

Ms. Madden (Classroom application 6.3) asks her class to design a game involving prime and composite numbers from 1 to 100 and to include directions.

One group designed this game: Put all numerals from 0 to 100 in a bag. Students form two teams of five members. Each team is given a Prime Number, Composite Number, or Neither label and stands them up. A student from each team takes turns drawing a number from the bag and placing it behind the corresponding label. The team with the total number of correct answers wins. Students who draw 0 or 1 must explain why they do not belong behind the Prime Number or Composite Number but behind the Neither label. (Though there is approximately a 4/1 ratio of composite to prime numbers from 2 to 100, each student has the same chance of drawing one of them.)

Students can *play games* that reinforce content.

Classroom application 6.11

After Ms. Henry teaches her classes the relationship among cups, pints, and quarts (Classroom application 5.19), she has them reinforce that content by playing a game using representative material. Several students are chosen to wear a string necklace with one paper cutout of correspondingly graduated cups, pints, or quarts. Another student wears a necklace of a paper cutout of the equal sign. These students come to the front of the room. The teacher puts several expressions on the board followed by the equal sign.

   2 cups =
   4 cups =
   2 pints =
   1 quart =
   1 pint =

For each expression, a different remaining student arranges the students wearing the symbols in the front of the room so that the symbols on both sides of the equal sign will make a "living" equation. Then that student completes the expression on the board to form a written equation.

Classroom application 6.12

Ms. Olinsky has her class play arithmetic Bingo. Instead of having the students cover cards with specific numerals represented by digits 1 to 75, the cards display addition, subtraction, multiplication, or division facts that equal numbers from 1 to 75. For example, B1 can be covered by 1 + 0, 0 + 1, 5 ÷ 5, 1 x 1, 1 ÷ 1, etc. G60 can be covered by 5 x 12, 4 x 15, 60 + 0, 60 ÷ 1, 120 ÷ 2, 60 - 0, etc.

Students first make 15 different equivalent values that represent totals from each group, B 1–15, I 16–30, N 31–45, G 46–60, O 61–75. Then they make different cards that contain a random selection of five totals from each group. When they finally play the game, students must do the mental calculation to determine whether a math fact can be covered when a number is called. This activity affords a more challenging way to reinforce arithmetic facts to make students more proficient.

ERROR ANALYSIS

Just as error analysis is used to give feedback to students (Chapter 4), students can *identify errors* to reinforce learning.

Classroom application 6.13

After grammar and spelling lessons, Mr. Wallace has his students write paragraphs with deliberate errors in grammar and spelling and place the paragraphs on the whiteboard. Other students must identify and correct the errors.

MNEMONICS

Other ways to provide connections (pathways) in the brain to reinforce learning are through mnemonics, techniques to improve memory. However, mnemonics are effective *only after the original learning is understood*. If not, it becomes rote memory, which is inefficient.

Classroom application 6.14

After Mr. Pastor taught his students the formula for the circumference of a circle by discovery (Classroom application 5.21) and when he was sure that they understood it, he gave them the rhyme

> Twinkle twinkle little star,
> Circumference equals $2\pi r$,
> It can also be πd,
> It's as easy as can be.

Mr. Pastor is aware that memorizing the formula and the rhyme without first *understanding* the formula makes it easy to forget.

Another reinforcing memory technique, mnemonic, is providing an acronym, a word formed by the first letters of terms involved in a series. Common examples of acronyms are the names of the spaces on the G-clef, FACE (in succession) and the names of the Great Lakes, (Huron, Ontario, Michigan, Erie, Superior), HOMES.

Besides acronyms, sentences can be used to help recall information. You are probably already familiar with the sentence, or some variation of it, used to remember the planets in order of distance from the sun, My very excellent mother just started unwrapping neat packages, correspondingly for Mercury, Venus, Earth, Mars, Jupiter, Saturn, Uranus, Neptune, and Pluto, and the sentence to recall the lines on the G-clef, Every good boy deserves fudge (or fun), for EGBDF.

Jingles, music, and rhymes can also be employed. Multiplication Rock was designed to help students remember single-digit multiplication. To remember the number of days in each month you probably learned a variation of

> Thirty days has September,
> April, June, and November.
> All the rest have 31 except February
> Which alone has 28 and one day more
> When leap year comes one year in four.

Any connection mnemonics can make between new material and what students already know will increase (reinforce) understanding and, therefore, memory.

Classroom application 6.15

Ms. Nathan is teaching spelling. Her class reads a story about a whippoorwill and will have to write about it. She helps the students remember how to spell whippoorwill by teaching them that the word can be put together by combining three words with which they are already familiar—whip, poor, and will.

Reinforcement can be improved by making connections (associations) to distinguish between words commonly used but frequently spelled incorrectly, such as principal/principle and hear/here. The princi*pal* (a person) is your *pal* and you h*ear* with your *ear*. The difference in spelling between desert and dessert is remembered by associating the double s in dessert with strawberry shortcake. Students who have difficulty remembering how to spell separate as either seperate or sep*ara*te should make the connection that "there is *a rat* in sep*ara*te."

PROCEDURAL AND SEMANTIC KNOWLEDGE

Another educational implication of using reinforcement and practice is understanding the difference between procedural and semantic knowledge. Procedural knowledge is "knowing how" to do something such as divide fractions or clean a carburetor—it is knowledge in action.

Procedural knowledge must be demonstrated. When faced with a fraction to divide, the student must divide correctly. "Students demonstrate procedural knowledge when they translate a passage into Spanish, correctly categorize a geometric shape, or craft a coherent paragraph" (Woolfolk, 2008, p. 280). Typing, making a bed, taking a shower, playing a musical instrument, and driving a car are also examples of procedural knowledge.

Rote rehearsal, reinforcing by practicing the same way over and over again, is appropriate for most types of procedural knowledge. Most of school learning, however, does not cover procedural but concerns semantic knowledge, that which involves *meaning*.

Because procedural knowledge can be taught and reinforced by rote, many teachers make the consistent error of teaching and reinforcing semantic knowledge also by rote. A typical example of learning by rote is evidenced by completing a course and several weeks later remembering very little. Unfortunately, this is a very common experience. To encode and retrieve semantic knowledge, it should be learned through *elaborative rehearsal*.

Wolfe (2001a) informed us that we are competing with a brain that was designed for survival, a brain that has kept us safe from predators. Schoolwork, though important for cultural survival, is not important to the brain for physical protection.

LeDoux (1996) has demonstrated that with a brain that is programmed to forget what is not critical to survival, namely, the content we learn in school, we are at the mercy of our elaborations. Therefore, if we do not elaboratively rehearse, we will forget. Elaborative rehearsal makes learning meaningful, especially personally meaningful, by creating connections to what we already know, and reinforcing the information in several *different* ways.

Classroom application 6.16

Ms. Chambers is constantly trying to grow professionally. She is aware of the fact that vocabulary development is extremely important in reading comprehension and to success in achieving the Common Core State Standards (Academic Vocabulary Builds Student Achievement, 2012; Sparks, 2013).

When she was a student, her teachers provided her with a list of vocabulary words. She had to look them up in a dictionary and write a sentence for each. Afterwards, she took a test on the vocabulary words and subsequently forgot most of them. She was not satisfied with this procedure. There had to be a better way to have her students understand and remember what the words *mean* (semantic knowledge).

Ms. Chambers listened to a tape about teaching vocabulary (Wolfe, 2001b), a method that was reported to increase vocabulary retention 200 percent. She decided to use the suggestions she gleaned from this tape and prior readings to teach vocabulary.

Ms. Chambers gave each of her students a *different* word. She selected the words carefully, using those that would come up in complex texts her students would be reading. She first taught her students how to guess or predict the meanings of words through context clues she presented in sentences and then through morphological strategies.

When finally presented with an individual word, the students were to first guess what the word may mean, then the choice of writing the dictionary definition or one found on the Internet, followed by a definition in their own words, one that made sense to them. Next the students were to use a second modality by creating a visual (picture, diagram) of what that word meant to them *personally*. This visual was to be followed by writing the word in a sentence and then writing the word in another sentence in a new context to deepen meaning. All of the above was then put on a vocabulary poster after which each student would present and discuss his/her poster in class.

The posters were subsequently displayed around the room. Students were encouraged to create vocabulary games such as crossword puzzles, Scrabble, vocabulary Bingo, or any other game to reinforce these same words.

When Ms. Chambers administered a subsequent test on these vocabulary words, she was thrilled that the average grade was 94 percent. After teaching other groups of words, Ms. Chambers interjected on the test words that were taught in prior weeks. Much to her surprise (and pleasure), the students retained, to a substantial degree, the meanings of the words.

TRANSFER

Learning can be reinforced by transferring (applying) learning to new situations.

Classroom application 6.17

Mr. Wallace (Classroom application 6.13) wants to keep his students aware of correct grammar and word usage. After they find deliberate errors in their peers' paragraphs, Mr. Wallace has his students watch different TV programs and make a note of incorrect grammar of the hosts/participants/reporters. Students then present and discuss these examples in class.

Some of the errors the students identified were:

The media is responsible for . . .
Between you and I, the mayor . . .
You should have went to see . . .
The criteria is going to be . . .
Me and my colleague went to see . . .
The reason Senator Jackson wrote this memo was because he . . .
He told more jokes than me.
She has a ways to go before she . . .
Now with regards to the budget, the congressman . . .
There are less calories in this cheesecake because it is made with . . .

The students seemed to enjoy "catching" these communication professionals in these errors. Mr. Wallace gave his students the voluntary assignment of informing the TV stations of the incorrect grammar.

DRAMA/ROLE PLAYING

Drama/role playing can be used effectively to reinforce learning.

Classroom application 6.18

Ms. Harvey's class has just read and discussed *To Kill a Mockingbird*. She is aware that drama involves students emotionally, so she asks her students to identify a scene that was particularly vivid for them. Students collaborate in groups to turn that scene into a script where students are subsequently assigned different roles to play. Students then indicate how they felt as they were playing that role, how that feeling was communicated by the words in the script, and how that feeling might be changed by selecting different words.

Ms. Harvey also has her younger students play roles after they read a short story or other literature including complex texts. Students can improvise or actually write the scripts in which they will participate.

Whenever a situation arises in Ms. Harvey's classes where students show insensitivity to the feelings of others, she assigns roles to the insensitive students where they receive the offending situation (stimulus).

Classroom application 6.19

After studying the circulatory system, Mr. Stevenson had his fourth-grade students watch a video on the circulatory system. Then he implemented a strategy that he had read about (Franklin, 2006).

Mr. Stevenson took his students to the gym. He had them act out the circulatory system by giving them red and blue ribbons, and having the students form lines which moved in the same path that blood flowed through the body.

Classroom application 6.20

Whenever Ms. Aviles completes a unit in history, she always has her students write a skit depicting a major event in that unit and then has them act out the skit. The students are given the choice of writing the skit in small groups or individually.

CHANGING THE BRAIN

Neuroscientists state that teachers could be brain changers. Teachers can help their students' long-term memories by returning to the new learning and building upon it. Developing long-term memory is not a linear one-stop experience but rather a continual process (Pillars, 2012).

Students need time to process information. Also, neuroscientists have advanced the primacy-recency effect which asserts that new information that is presented at the beginning of a lesson has the optimal chance of being recalled (due to primacy); the information presented last in a lesson has the next best chance of being recalled (due to recency). About every 20 minutes, there should be some kind of review or consolidation of information presented (Pillars, 2012).

Classroom application 6.21

Mr. Spano makes it a point to avoid traditional activities at the beginning of class. These include reviewing prior learning, making announcements, discussing homework, and taking attendance, leaving those activities to after the peak learning time (primacy) has occurred. Instead, he begins his lessons by presenting most of the information in the first 10 minutes of class. Mr. Spano then spends time reviewing the content by asking higher-level questions, making sure that he gives his students enough time to both process the questions and come up with a response. During the review he tries to continually make connections between the new learning and what his students already know. During the last 10 minutes (recency) he introduces additional important information. The students then synthesize the information presented in the lesson.

HOMEWORK

Many teachers assign *homework* to reinforce what was studied in class. There is abundant research supporting both more and less homework with parents complaining either way. The greatest support for homework is that there is a positive relationship between homework and standardized-test performance (DeNisco, 2013).

But most research concludes "that carefully planning homework helps students to master basic rules, increase skill speed, deepen understanding of concepts and prepare for subsequent learning. Teachers should strive to match the type of homework given to the learning goal to make homework a focused learning experience" (Wind, 2012, p. 4). It is, therefore, beneficial to place at the top of the homework assignment the learning objective or goal.

The controversy over homework has resulted in having different policies in different school districts. These policies range from assigning no homework at all to assigning no homework on weekends to provide downtime, or designating a specific amount of time to be allotted for each subject.

A problem occurs when students have different opportunities for doing homework. Do students have a quiet place to work? Does the parent or guardian follow through to ensure that homework will be done? Does the parent or guardian have the interest or ability to assist with homework?

A general principle that has been implemented in assigning homework is multiplying the grade level of the student by 10 minutes to determine the appropriate amount of homework time to be assigned each night. Some suggest that by the time a student reaches the end of high school, two hours should be allotted each night to prepare for college workloads.

As with any other assignment, if homework is to be assigned, the homework should be *meaningful*, not busywork.

Classroom application 6.22

To keep his students focused, Mr. Grainger always puts the objective of the homework on top of the assignment. Whenever possible, he gives the student a choice regarding which one they will do. A typical assignment looks like this:
Objective: To compute the volume of a cylinder
Choose one of the following:

1. Find three objects in your house that are cylinders. Draw a diagram of them, labeling what they are, their dimensions, and volume. Be sure to use the proper units.
2. Complete the first three problems on page 78 in your textbook. Then rewrite the problems so that all the dimensions in each problem will be of *different* units. Complete the problems with the new units.
3. Write three cylinder problems for your classmates. Vary the information provided in each problem so that your classmates may have to find the actual volume or, given the volume and one other measurement, will have to find the third.

SELF-REFLECTION

- On which occasions have you modeled new learning?
- How have you and your students applied the law of distributed practice?

Strengthening and Deepening New Learning

- Give some examples of some reinforcing assignments you believe your students found meaningful.
- How has learning been summarized in your classes? Did you, the students, or both of you do the summarizing?
- How was original content you taught subsequently viewed in new ways?
- How have you used games relevant to the maturity/developmental level of your students?
- What have you done to help students analyze their own errors?
- How have you used mnemonics?
- What content connections have you used to enhance learning?
- How have you used elaborative rehearsal to strengthen learning?
- Give some examples of how you had your students apply new learning to different situations.
- How have you used visuals to reinforce learning?
- What have you taught recently that could have been reinforced by drama?
- How do you intend to use the primacy/recency effect in future learning?
- If you assign homework, what evidence can you present that the homework is meaningful?

Appendix A

Involving Students in Active Learning

A Case Study

It was well publicized that Rahm Emanuel, while chief of staff for President Barack Obama, said, "You never want a serious crisis to go to waste." Though he meant this politically, you can examine how it would apply to education.

Read the following case study regarding how a crisis was handled to actively involve the whole school in implementing learning theory. As you read through the case study, think of a current crisis or any other event that has learning potential to see how you could apply the same or similar examples in your classroom/school.

The year was 1979. Mr. Parker, a teacher at a suburban high school, driving to work one morning, decided that he had had enough. What irritated him was not so much the fact that several times he had to wait in line for over an hour to buy gasoline. It was not even that he had paid almost $1.50 per gallon with the prospect of paying $2.00 or higher that bothered him. Nor was he aggravated by the $100 billion dollars a year that the United States paid to oil-producing countries. What really provoked him into wanting to do something about the gasoline situation was that it seemed out of his control. He was neither a politician nor an oil company executive. He was an educator. What could he do? He could not control supplies, production, or price. All that was within his power was to try to conserve.

As he pulled into the school parking lot, still stewing over his plight, there was spread out before him a conspicuous example of wasted gasoline—the cars of students who could just as well ride the school bus. What was in the

American parents' psyches that made them feel that their sixteen-year-olds had a God-given right to an automobile?

He began to see the cause that youth needed. Could he motivate this "me generation" into saving gasoline? After considerable thought he concluded that, if students were really to conserve gasoline, they would have to be convinced intellectually and emotionally of the necessity. They probably would be convinced more by their peers than by their teachers or parents, and the decision to conserve would have to originate from the students themselves. What was needed was a nurturing environment that would trigger this decision.

Mr. Parker waited for the opportune moment. He saw it when OPEC once again boosted its prices, and gasoline at the pumps followed with a 10-cent per gallon increase. He called leaders from the "worms," "nerds," "heads," and "jocks" to join him for lunch. At first they chatted about school. As part of the conversation, Mr. Parker casually mentioned how the gasoline problem was affecting the economy. Before long the students were verbalizing their concern about the gasoline situation. They asked him what he thought could be done. He responded that as citizens and consumers, they, as well as he, currently lacked the knowledge to make informed decisions, but if they wanted to study the situation, he would be willing to help. The students expressed the feeling that the gasoline problem was only a small part of the entire energy emergency, and its nature was so critical that some cooperative effort should be made within the school to attempt a comprehensive approach.

The group requested a meeting with department heads to explore the possibility of setting up an interdisciplinary program to inform the students about each aspect of the energy crisis. When their request was granted, these representative students and others they invited met with the chairpersons, the student council president, the principal, and his assistant. The students felt important sharing their concerns and offering suggestions. After considerable interaction, all departments decided to incorporate into their curricula a separate phase of the energy problem. As each chairperson described how the energy situation could be viewed from his/her own discipline, the ideas served as a catalyst to activate other departments to support or enhance the content.

By the end of that meeting, the social studies chairperson agreed to consider the history, geography, and politics of the Middle East. Students would study the economic aspects of the gasoline situation and see how it related to trade, the dollar, and inflation. They would explore the role of government, the Department of Energy, oil companies, auto manufacturers, and consumers.

The math and science departments volunteered to send for energy education materials available from the Clearinghouse on Science, Mathematics, and Environmental Education from the National Science Teachers' Association. They would spend time exploring oil formation, location, and excavating as well as considering other forms of energy and energy terms such as the BTU and resistance. Annual reports obtained from oil companies would serve to introduce concepts from statistics, accounting, and probability. Graphs from the reports would be analyzed.

The English department chairperson felt that themes relating to energy could be the central topics in the teaching of essay and poetry writing. Contributions of the students would be published in the school newspaper. Quizzes and crossword puzzles dealing with energy vocabulary could be constructed. An all-out effort would be made to find articles, short stories, novels, mysteries and adventure stories related to oil. Interested students were encouraged to collaborate to write and produce a play on the topic of energy.

Art, home economics, and social studies offered their assistance in designing sets and costumes for the English department's play. Physical education suggested a "Run for Energy" with the proceeds going to renting energy films. Art also volunteered to have the students prepare collages, models, dioramas, posters, cartoons, and comics with energy themes. Together with Industrial Arts they would guide the students in analyzing the school building and their own homes and apartments for energy efficiency, making recommendations for improvements and learning to draw house plans and interiors that were more energy efficient.

The music department decided to "set a tone" by collecting records on energy to be played in the cafeteria. Students offered "Gallon of Gas" by the Kinks and "Fun, Fun, Fun (Till Her Daddy Takes the T-Bird Away)" by the Beach Boys as popular records. Students could compose songs to any poetry produced in the English classes and write energy lyrics to rock songs.

Believing that faculty involvement was essential to setting an example for students, the music director stated that she would enlist faculty for a concert to launch the energy activities. In order to show how the energy problem was interconnected with other areas of the economy, the faculty would perform a disco version of "Dry Bones" with energy-related lyrics and sing the rock songs with the new lyrics.

Though these suggestions were by no means exhaustive, they did represent a beginning. The group agreed to hold a planning session each week to follow through with these initial suggestions and assess progress. These sessions would be open to any interested students, faculty, administrators or parents. The principal offered a room to serve as an energy center manned by the students.

As weeks passed, the students were immersed in energy. Many events and activities took place. A specifically selected team from the local Automobile Club was invited to present an assembly. For the first time, students learned to identify the parts of the internal combustion engine, their location and function—information that affected all of them but was not even required on their driver's test. The team asked how many students took their cars to school. From the large show of hands, the team calculated how much gasoline students were using and translated this information into specific data concerning how rich they were making OPEC.

The students were quick to justify taking their cars to school. The buses were uncomfortable. Seniors had no early nor late classes and did not want to "hang out." Students wanted to go out to lunch because they did not like the food in the cafeteria and enjoyed driving around during a free period. They liked the freedom and sense of control that "wheels" gave them. A group of students had to go to work or participate in sports after school. Some students admitted that "other kids" liked to show off. The team listed these elicited reasons on a blackboard and then invited suggestions from the student body regarding how to handle each one.

Shortly, the ideas flowed. Why couldn't the board of education see to it that the buses were kept clean and warm? A student group could organize campaigns for preventing littering on school buses and set up a rotating group of students to help clean the buses. Maybe the cleaning of the buses could be part of detention! Special enrichment, remedial, or just entertaining programs might be set up for those who had free periods or no early or late classes. Exercise classes, music listening, peer tutoring, special films, guest speakers, instructional modules, interesting labs, collectors' clubs were just a few suggestions.

A concerted effort could be made to improve the cafeteria food. It needed improvement in the varieties of offerings and in nutritional value. Students could make their own lunch or prepare creative lunches for others. And, they asked themselves, how long would students have real freedom and control if OPEC were able to control production and price? The team emphasized over and over all that was needed to break the oil cartel's back was a 10 percent reduction in oil imports. The students agreed, many of them reluctantly, that 10 percent was not overwhelming and that they really should try to save gas. They would begin by surveying driving habits and drawing up a comprehensive plan to maximize car use.

After the assembly, arrangements were made with the Auto Club to leave a model of the internal combustion engine in the school for a few weeks. Arrangements were also made for the team from the Auto Club to return to the school to present an assembly on driving conservation. Here, students learned the value of combining trips, accelerating smoothly, keeping efficient speeds of 40 to 50 miles per hour, regularly checking spark-plug points, wheel alignment, oil and water. Students were informed how to save gasoline by minimizing resistance through keeping tires properly inflated, closing windows and substituting vents at high speeds on the highway, removing unnecessary weights from the trunk, and avoiding permanent roof racks. The waste for not doing any of the above was transformed by the team into data that affected the students' wallets.

The students became more and more tuned into the energy problem. Energy became the topic of conversation during lunch, after school, and over the telephone. The students tried to motivate more and more of their peers into conserving energy. A life-size cartoon entitled "Cool Wastes Fuel" was placed on the wall inside the main entrance to the school. The cartoon depicted two sheiks driving in a Mercedes convertible laden with gold coins. The sheiks were laughing at some faceless high school students who were filling their tanks at a gasoline pump. Each day, through the courtesy of the Photography Club, blown-up pictures of students who regularly drove their cars to school were superimposed on the blank faces.

The students were not satisfied with just pressuring their peers but attempted to involve the entire community. A group translated the driving conservation information they obtained from the assembly presented by the Auto Club onto posters which were placed strategically throughout the town. Students asked the local library to prepare an energy exhibit and make available a collection of books, magazines, and pamphlets on the subject. The library, in turn, sponsored a film series selected from the Energy Films Interim Catalog made available by the Department of Energy and prepared a list of free energy materials along with addresses for obtaining the materials.

The Future Teachers' Club at the high school planned and presented energy learning activities for the junior high and elementary school pupils to make them more energy conscious. The Guidance Office presented an energy-related career night. A local bank was asked by the students to add bicycles to its list of free gifts for new accounts and to open a "branch" called the Idea Bank, a fancy name for a suggestion box, to be placed in a conspicuous location in the main window for the purpose of soliciting energy-saving suggestions from the community. Local merchants were requested to support the school program by offering free gifts to the contributors of the best suggestions from the Idea Bank and to use shopping bags that said "Save Energy."

The students got the president of the board of education to arrange an interview between three students and the mayor who, in turn, arranged an interview between the students and the governor. The students were interested in determining what was being done at the local and state levels regarding the energy problem. One of the governor's representatives, along with representatives from an oil company, a public utility, a consumer group, and an operator of a local gasoline station, accepted an invitation to participate in a panel discussion on energy that was held at the high school and open to the community.

The public was invited to attend a workshop on coping with energy shortages and inflation sponsored by the Psychology Club and to view the play that was eventually written, acted, and directed by the English classes. The social studies department contacted the League of Women Voters for the purpose of preparing and distributing pamphlets summarizing present officeholders' policies on energy matters. The league also agreed to summarize for publication the energy views of candidates for public office.

A small group of research-oriented students designed a questionnaire to get information on energy-saving habits of a random sample of community members. The students programmed the school computer to process the information. And when the results of the questionnaire convinced the students that the community was still cavalier with respect to energy conservation, they began to keep weekly records of the gasoline sold in seven local stations. The students got the mayor's permission to construct a graph in the center of town to record the weekly consumption of gasoline in these seven stations. The goal was to reduce gasoline purchasing by 10 percent in 10 weeks. A symbol of OPEC with its back broken was placed on the 10th week.

A local newspaper reporter, sensing a story, visited the high school. She was so impressed that she decided to publish the questionnaire results, write a weekly article telling what was being accomplished by the students, and help the research group organize an energy education blitz to get the cooperation of the community for the gasoline cut. She even got her paper to reproduce the graph each week.

The students at the high school, encouraged by their success, decided to contact the leadership of other high schools in the area to see if students there would be willing to undertake similar projects. The articles written by the reporter caught the attention of other media. Local radio and TV stations repeatedly interviewed the students, administration, and members of the board of education. As other schools became involved, their activities were also advertised by the media.

Several nationally broadcast TV shows invited students who had originated the energy conservation plan to appear as guests. Schools throughout the country began to contact the TV stations to find out how they could institute similar energy programs. One of the largest game manufacturers in the United States heard about the students' activities and offered a $10,000 prize plus royalties to a group of students who could devise a marketable energy game. Several universities and corporations got together to offer engineering scholarships to students who could design energy-saving mechanisms and science scholarships to students who could create practical synthetic fuels.

Within several months there developed a dramatic reduction in oil consumption. The resulting oil glut forced OPEC to lower prices. There was a corresponding drop of 2 percent in the rate of inflation.

The principal and chairpersons had never observed such enthusiasm on the part of students. Absenteeism, vandalism, and drug and alcohol use declined. Students were involved firsthand with learning how to obtain and use information. Many students who had never even spoken to each other were working together. The faculty was more stimulated than they had been in years. What was even more surprising is that some teachers who were considered "burnouts" tried innovative teaching. All involved agreed to look for other crises and problems that could be capitalized upon to replicate and expand the learning activities used in attacking the energy shortage.

References

Academic vocabulary builds student achievement. (2012, November). *Education Update, 54*(11), 1, 4. Alexandria, VA: Association for Supervision and Curriculum Development.
Ashcraft, M. (2002). *Cognition* (3rd ed.) Upper Saddle River, NJ: Prentice Hall.
Baddeley, A. (2007). *Working memory, thought, and action*. London: Oxford University Press.
Bright, N. (2012). *Those who can: Why master teachers do what they do*. Lanham, MD: Rowman & Littlefield.
Brookhart, S. (2012, September). Preventing feedback fizzle. *Educational Leadership, 70*(1), 24–29.
Brooks, D. (2011). *The social animal: The hidden sources of love, character, and achievement*. New York: Random House.
Brophy, J. E. (1988). On motivating students. In D. Berliner & B. Rosenshine (Eds.), *Talks to teachers* (pp. 201–245). New York: Random House.
Caine, R. N., & Caine, G. (1994). *Making connections: Teaching and the human brain*. Menlo Park, CA: Addison Wesley.
Cangelosi, J. (2008). *Classroom management strategies: Gaining and maintaining students' cooperation* (6th ed.). Hoboken, NJ: John Wiley & Sons.
Canter, L. (2006). *Classroom management for academic success*. Bloomington, IN: Solution Tree.
Chetty, R., Friedman, J., & Rockoff, J. (2012, January). *The long-term impacts of teachers: Teacher value-added and student outcomes in adulthood* (NBER Working Paper No. 17699, JEL No. I2, J24).
Cole, J. (2012). *Teaching the way students learn: Practical applications for today's classrooms*. Lanham, MD: Rowman & Littlefield.
Cotton, K. (2000). *The schooling practices that matter most*. Alexandria, VA: Association for Supervision and Curriculum Development.
Covington, M. V. (1992). *Making the grade: A self-worth perspective on motivation and school reform*. New York: Cambridge University Press.
Csikszentmihalyi, M. (1990). *Flow: The psychology of optimal experience*. New York: Harper & Row.
Cummings, C. (2000). *Winning strategies for classroom management*. Alexandria, VA: Association for Supervision and Curriculum Development.
Curwin, R., Mendler, A., & Mendler, B. (2008). *Discipline with dignity: New challenges, new solutions* (3rd ed.). Alexandria, VA: Association for Supervision and Curriculum Development.
Deci, E. L., & Ryan, R. M. (1985). *Intrinsic motivation and self-determination in human behavior*. New York: Plenum.

DeNisco, A. (2013, March). Homework or not? That is the (research) question. *District Administration.*

Duffy, F. (2013, February 22). Teaching resource watch: Financial lessons for kids. Teaching Now. *Education Week* blogs. http://blogs.edweek.org/teachers/teaching_now/2013/02/teaching_resource_watch_financial_lessons_for_kids.html.

Dvorkin, H. (2012, August 6). Lack of education linked to record levels of debt. *Fox Latino News*, p. 14.

Elias, M. (2013, January 16). Helping students set goals and find success. *Edutopia.* http://www.edutopia.org/blog/students-set-goals-find-success-maurice-elias

Emmer, E., Evertson, C., & Worsham, M. (2003a). *Classroom management for elementary teachers* (6th ed.). Boston: Allyn & Bacon.

Emmer, E., Evertson, C., & Worsham, M. (2003b). *Classroom management for secondary teachers* (6th ed.). Boston: Allyn & Bacon.

Engel, S., & Sandstrom, M. (2010, July 22). There's only one way to stop a bully. *The New York Times*, p. A23.

Erwin, J. (2004). *The classroom of choice: Giving students what they need and getting what you want.* Alexandria, VA: Association for Supervision and Curriculum Development.

Felch, J., Song, J., & Poindexter, S. (2010, December 22). In reforming schools, quality of teaching often overlooked. *Los Angeles Times*, p. 4.

Ferlazzo, L. (2012, August 16). Response: Don't wait until Christmas to smile---Clasroom Q & A. *Education Week* blogs. http://blogs.edweek.org/teachers/classroom_qa_with_larry_ferlazzo/2012/08/response_dont_wait_until_christmas_to_smile.html.

Franklin, J. (June, 2006). Mental mileage: How teachers are putting brain research to use. *Education Update, 47*(6). Alexandria, VA: Association for Supervision and Curriculum Development.

Frisby, B., & Martin, M. (2010, April). Instructor-student and student-student rapport in the classroom. *Communication Education, 59*(2), 146–164.

Gammill, A. (2010, May 21). *IPS teacher goes from mutiny to best in class.* Indystar.com.

Gewertz, C. (2008, October 15). States press ahead on "21st-century skills." *Education Week*, (28) 8, 21, 23.

Gewertz, C. (2012, April 11). Do you know how effective your instructional materials are? *Education Week* blogs. http://blogs.edweek.org/edweek/curriculum/2012/04/a_call_for_research_on_effecti.html.

Ginsburg, D. (2012, August 6). The effect of affect. *Education Week* blogs. http://blogs.edweek.org/teachers/coach_gs_teaching_tips/2012/08/the_effect_of_affect_1.html.

Goleman, D. (1998). *Working with emotional intelligence.* New York: Bantam Books.

Good, T., & Brophy, J. (2003). *Looking in classrooms* (9th ed.). Boston: Allyn & Bacon.

Hanushek, E. (2011, April 6). Recognizing the value of good teachers. *Education Week, 30*(27), 34–35.

Haycock, K. (1998). Good teaching matters . . . a lot. *Thinking K–16, 3*(2), 1–14.

Heiten, L. (2013, January 16). Research review: Teacher expectations matter. Teacher blogs, Teaching Now, *Education Week Teacher.* http://blogs.edweek.org/teachers/teaching_now/2013/01/research_review_teacher_expectations_matter.html.

Hudson, K. (2013, February 14). Smithsonian launches quests program to encourage discovery and collaboration. *The Journal*, Project-Based Learning/News.

Hunter, R. (2004). *Madeline Hunter's mastery teaching: Increasing instructional effectiveness in elementary and secondary schools* (Rev. ed.). Thousand Oaks, CA: Corwin Press.

Isselhardt, E. (2013, February 11). Creating school-wide PBL aligned to common core. *Edutopia.* http://www.edutopia.org/blog/PBL-aligned-to-common-core-eric-isslehardt.

Jensen, E. (1998). *Teaching with the brain in mind.* Alexandria, VA: Association for Supervision and Curriculum Development.

Jensen, E. (2005). *Teaching with the brain in mind* (2nd ed.). Alexandria, VA: Association for Supervision and Curriculum Development.

Jones, V. F., & Jones, L. S. (2003). *Comprehensive classroom management: Creating communities of support and solving problems* (7th ed.). Boston: Allyn & Bacon.

Joyce, B., & Showers, B. (2002). *Student achievement through staff development* (3rd ed.). Alexandria, VA: Association for Supervision and Curriculum Development.

Joyce, B., Weil, M., & Calhoun, E. (2004). *Models of teaching* (7th ed.). Boston: Pearson.

Kadlec, D. (2013, February 22). The best way to teach kids about money? Slip it into math and English classes. *Time: Business and Money*. http://business.time.com/2013/02/22/the-best-way-to-teach-kids-about-money-slip-it-into-math-and-english-classes/.

Kaufman, D., & Moss, D. (2010, April). A new look at preservice teachers' conceptions of classroom management and organization: Uncovering complexity and dissonance. *The Teacher Educator, 45*(2), 118–136.

Kendall, J. & Marzano, R. (2011). Content knowledge: A compendium of standards and benchmarks for K-12 education. (Electronic version). http://www2.mcrel.org/compendium/browse.asp.

Kohn, A. (1996). *Beyond discipline: From compliance to community*. Alexandria, VA: Association for Supervision and Curriculum Development.

Kolis, M., & Krusack, E. (2012). *Powerful ideas in teaching: Creating environments in which students want to learn*. Lanham, MD: Rowman & Littlefield.

Laster, M. (2007). *Brain-based teaching for all subjects: Patterns to promote learning*. Lanham, MD: Rowman & Littlefield.

LeDoux, J. (1996). *The emotional brain: The mysterious underpinnings of emotional life*. New York: Simon & Schuster.

Lyubomirsky, S. (2012, December 2). New love: A short shelf life. *The New York Times Sunday Review*, p. 1, 4.

Marks, M. (2000, January 9). Education Life. *The New York Times*, pp. 16–17.

Marzano, R. (2003). *What works in schools*. Alexandria, VA: Association for Supervision and Curriculum Development.

Marzano, R. (2007). *The art and science of teaching: A comprehensive framework for effective instruction*. Alexandria, VA: Association for Supervision and Curriculum Development.

Marzano, R. (2011, March). Relating to students: It's what you do that counts. *Educational Leadership*, 68(6), 82–83.

Maslow, A. (1968). *Toward a psychology of being* (2nd ed.). New York: Van Nostrand.

Maslow, A. (1970). *Motivation and personality* (2nd ed.). New York: Harper & Row.

McLeod, J., Fisher, J., & Hoover, G. (2003). *The key elements of classroom management: Managing time and space, student behavior, and instructional strategies*. Alexandria, VA: Association for Supervision and Curriculum Development.

Meier, D. (2012, December 13). How disrespect hurts kids. *Education Week* blogs. http://blogs.edweek.org/edweek/Bridging-Differences/2012/12/_the_argument_ought_not.html.

Mendler, A. (2013, March 14). Climate control: Six ways to improve your school environment. *Edutopia*. http://www.edutopia.org/blog/climate-improve-your-school-environment-allen-mendler.

Mumford, M. D., Costanza, D. P., Baughman, W. A., Threlfall, V., & Fleishman, E. A. (1994). Influence of abilities on performance during practice: Effects of massed and distributed practice. *Journal of Educational Psychology*, (86) 134–144.

National Commission on Teaching and America's Future. (1996). *What matters most: Teaching for America's future*. New York: Carnegie Foundation, Author.

Nielsen, L. (2012, September 10). Enriching literacy with cell phones: 3 ideas to get started. *Smart Brief*. SmartBlogs on Education. http://smartblogs.com/education/2012/09/10/enriching-literacy-cell-phones-3-ideas-get-started/.

Nightingale, J. (2006, June 20). Whiteboards under the microscope. *Education Guardian*, p. 2–3.

Nuthall, G. (1999). The way students learn: Acquiring knowledge from an integrated science and social studies unit. *Elementary School Journal, 99*(4), 303–341.

Nuthall, G., & Alton-Lee, A. (1993). Predicting learning from student experience of teaching: A theory of student knowledge construction in classrooms. *American Educational Research Journal, 30*(4), 799–840.

Oakes, J., & Lipton, M. (2003). *Teaching to change the world* (2nd ed.). New York: McGraw-Hill.

Pagliaro, M. (2011). *Educator or bully?: Managing the 21st century classroom*. Lanham, MD: Rowman & Littlefield.

Pagliaro, M. (2012). *Mastery teaching skills: A resource for implementing the Common Core State Standards*. Lanham, MD: Rowman & Littlefield.

Piaget, J. (1954). *The construction of reality in the child*, (M. Cook, Trans.). New York: Basic Books.

Pillars, W. (2012, March 27). What neuroscience tells us about deepening learning. *Education Week Teacher*. http://www.edweek.org/tm/articles/2012/03/27/tln_pillars_neuroscience.html.

Pipho, C. (1998, January). The value-added side of standards. *Phi Delta Kappan*, pp. 341–42.

Resnick, L. B. (1987). *Education and learning to think*. Washington, DC: Academic Press.

Rinke, W. (1997, September). How to be a winner. *Family Circle*, p. 10.

Russert, T. (2001, May 20). Commencement address delivered at Dominican College, Orangeburg, NY.

Ryan, K., Cooper, J., & Tauer, S. (2008). *Teaching for student learning: Becoming a master teacher*. Boston: Houghton Mifflin.

Sanders, W., & Rivers, J. (1996). *Cumulative and residual effects of teachers on future student academic achievement*. Research progress report. Knoxville: University of Tennessee, Value-Added Research and Assessment Center.

Santelli, R. (2012, September 5). *Just how big is $1,000,000,000,000?* http://video.cnbc.com/gallery/?video=3000113951.

Secretary's Commission on Achieving Necessary Skills. (1991). *What work requires of schools: A SCANS report for America 2000*. U.S. Department of Labor, Author.

Sparks, S. (2013, February 6). Students must learn more words, say studies. *Education Week*, *32*(20), 1, 16–17.

Stansbury, M. (2006, March 21). "Learning replaces "teaching". *eSchool News*. http://www.eschoolnews.com/2008/03/21/learning-replaces-teaching/.

Steinberg, S. (2013, February 27). Educational technology: 7 ways to bring apps, gadgets, online services into school classrooms. *Huffington Post*. http://www.huffingtonpost.com/scott-steinberg/education-technology-7-wa_b_2758475.html.

Steiny, J. (2010, December 20). Teaching kids to learn the most from their mistakes. *The Providence Journal*. http://juliasteiny.files.wordpress.com/2011/07/12-12-2010-teaching-kids-to-learn-the-most-from-their-mistakes.pdf.

Stepien, W., Johnson, T., & Checkley, K. (1997). *Problem-based learning: Facilitator's guide*. Alexandria, VA: Association for Supervision and Curriculum Development.

Tan, S. (2013, February 16). Students pioneer the iPad frontier. *The Buffalo News*, p. 9.

Tips to help you flip your classroom (2013, February). *Education Update*, *55*(2), Author.

Waidelich, W. (2012, April 3). Engaging students…dangling the carrot. *Education Week* blogs. http://blogs.edweek.org/edweek/transforming_learning/2012/04/engaging_studentsdangling_the_carrot.html.

Wiggins, G. (1996, Spring). Achieving assessment with exemplars: Why students and teachers need models. *Gifted Child Quarterly*, 40(2), 66-6.

Wiggins, G., & McTighe, J. (1998). *Understanding by design*. Alexandria, VA: Association for Supervision and Curriculum Development.

Wiggins, G., & McTighe, J. (2005). *Understanding by design* (2nd ed.). Upper Saddle River, NJ: Prentice Hall.

Willingham, D. (2009). *Why don't students like school?* San Francisco: Jossey-Bass.

Wilson, L. (2006). *How students really learn: Instructional strategies that work*. Lanham, MD: Rowman & Littlefield.

Wind, K. (2012, November 25). Kingston school board studying homework policy. *Daily Freeman*, p. 12.

Wolfe, P. (2001a). Brain research: Fad or foundation? Audiotape #201099, Alexandria, VA: Association for Supervision and Curriculum Development.

Wolfe, P. (2001b). *Brain matters: Translating research into classroom practice*. Alexandria, VA: Association for Supervision and Curriculum Development.

Wolk, S. (2008, September). Joy in school. *Educational Leadership*, *60*(1), 8–15.

Wolpert-Gawron, H. (2012, April 30). Kids speak out on student engagement. *Edutopia*. http://www.edutopia.org/blog/student-engagement-stories-heather-wolpert-gawron.
Wong, H., & Wong, R. (1998). *The first days of school*. Mountain View, CA: Harry K. Wong Publications.
Wong, H. & Wong, R. (2005, September). Effective teaching. *Teachers Net Gazette*. http://teachers.net/wong/DEC10/.
Woolfolk, A. (2008). *Educational psychology* (10th ed.). Boston: Pearson Education.
Wright, S., Horn, S., & Sanders, W. (1997). Teacher and classroom context effects on student achievement: Implications for teacher evaluation. *Journal of Personnel Evaluation in Education*, 11, 57–67.

About the Author

Marie Pagliaro is currently a professional development consultant. She was a full professor and Director of the Teacher Education Division at Dominican College, Chair of the Education at Marymount College, a supervisor of student teachers at Lehman College of the City University of New York, and Chair of the Science Department and teacher of chemistry, general science, and mathematics in the Yonkers Public Schools. She received her Ph.D. in Curriculum and Teaching from Fordham University.

www.ingramcontent.com/pod-product-compliance
Lightning Source LLC
Chambersburg PA
CBHW052131300426
44116CB00010B/1853